RE-DISCOVERING
Medieval Realms

Other titles in this series:

THE SCHOOLS HISTORY PROJECT

S·H·P

OFFICIAL TEXT

RE-DISCOVERING
Medieval
Realms

BRITAIN 1066-1500

Colin Shephard
Alan Large

Series Editor:
Colin Shephard

Consultant Editor:
Terry Fiehn

JOHN MURRAY

The Schools History Project

This project was set up by the Schools Council in 1972. Its main aim was to suggest suitable objectives for history teachers, and to promote the use of appropriate materials and teaching methods for their realisation. This involved a reconsideration of the nature of history and its relevance in secondary schools, the design of a syllabus framework which shows the uses of history in the education of adolescents, and the setting up of appropriate examinations.

Since 1978 the project has been based at Trinity and All Saints' College, Leeds. It is now self-funding and with the advent of the National Curriculum it has expanded its publications to provide courses for Key Stage 3, and for a range of GCSE and A level syllabuses. The project provides INSET for all aspects of National Curriculum, GCSE and A level history. Its website can be found at www.tasc.ac.uk/shp

Words printed in SMALL CAPITALS are defined in the Glossary on page 104.

Note: The wording and sentence structure of some written sources have been adapted and simplified to make them accessible to all pupils, while faithfully perserving the sense of the original.

© Colin Shephard, Alan Large 1993 with revisions by Terry Fiehn 2000

First published in 1993 as *Discovering Medieval Realms* by John Murray (Publishers) Ltd, a member of the Hodder Headline Group
338 Euston Road,
London NW1 3BH

This completely revised edition first published 2000

Reprinted 2001 (twice), 2002 (twice), 2003, 2004

Layouts by Fiona Webb
Artwork by Countryside Illustrations, Linden Artists, Tony Randell, Steve Smith
Colour separations by Colourscript
Typeset in 11½/13pt Concorde by Wearset, Boldon, Tyne and Wear
Printed and bound in Dubai.

A catalogue entry for this title is available from the British Library

ISBN 0 7195 8542 2
Teachers' Resource Book ISBN 0 7195 8543 0

Contents

1066 The Battle of Hastings

1087 The Domesday Survey

1170 The murder of Becket

1000

1100

1200

SECTION 1
INTRODUCTION

1265 The siege of Kenilworth

1348 The Black Death

1381 The Peasants' Revolt

1300   1400   1500

What were the Middle Ages like?

▶▶ Some history books say that the Middle Ages were violent and dangerous. According to these books, there was war and killing; illness and disease; cruelty and superstition. Look at the paintings on pages 2–5 which come from the Middle Ages and see what you think.

▼ SOURCE 1

SOURCE 2 ▶

▼ SOURCE 3

▲ SOURCE 4

▼ ACTIVITY

1 In your own words, describe what is happening in each of the sources in Collection A. Here are some words that might help you:

coffins	burying	baiting	attacking
	witchcraft	goat	broomstick
bodies	hanging	looting	war

2 Which of the words below do you think best describe the Middle Ages as they are shown in Collection A?

violent	friendly	peaceful	caring
dark	dangerous	nasty	safe

3 If you were living in the Middle Ages which scene would make you most afraid? Explain why.
4 What chance would you have of living a peaceful, pleasant life?

▼ SOURCE 5

WHAT WERE THE MIDDLE AGES LIKE?

COLLECTION B

▼ ACTIVITY

1 Describe what you can see in Collection B. Use the words and phrases below to help you:

> hard-working
> skilled craftsmen
> nice buildings
> clever people   games
> peaceful   religious
> plenty of food to eat
> full of light

2 Which of these scenes would you most like to be in? Explain why.

3 How does this view of the Middle Ages differ from the one in Collection A?

▼ DISCUSS

4 You would have a very different view of the Middle Ages if you had only seen the paintings in Collection A. How does this help us to understand why we sometimes have different ideas about what the Middle Ages were like?

▼ YOUR QUESTIONS

5 Working in pairs, write down five questions you would like to ask about the Middle Ages.
Discuss your questions as a class and create a class list of questions. Keep them safe. You will need them later.

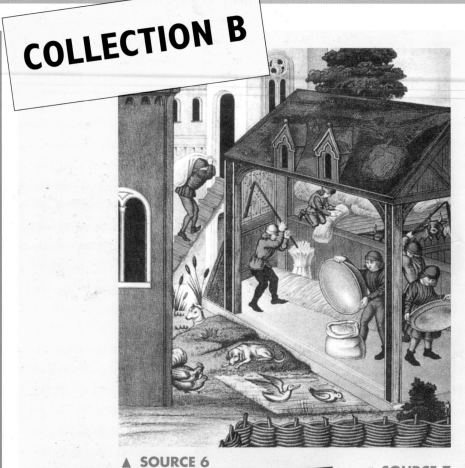

▲ SOURCE 6

◄ SOURCE 7

4 ▲

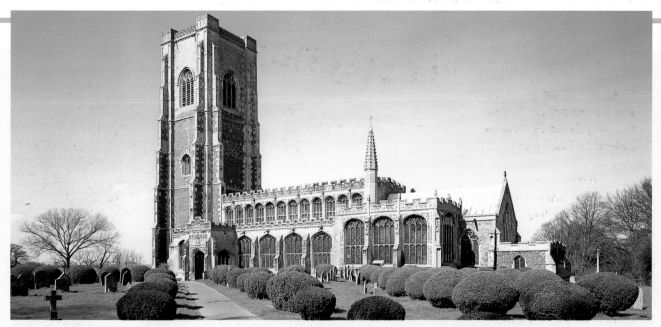

▲ SOURCE 8

▲ SOURCE 9

▲ SOURCE 10

Your pathway

In this book you will be finding out about life in MEDIEVAL times. The rest of this book is split into several sections.

Section 2: The Norman Conquest
This section tells you about the last time England was invaded, in 1066. After a fierce battle at Hastings, the English got a new king – William of Normandy. You will find out how William conquered the country and made the people obey him. You will also find out how he started to change things.

Section 3: Living in medieval times
This section tells you about different aspects of life in the Middle Ages. For example, you will find out about:

- how people lived in villages
- the work people had to do for the lord of the MANOR
- what people believed about God, Heaven and Hell
- the horrors of the Black Death.

Section 4: Problems facing medieval kings
It was not always easy being a king. People might try to get rid of you or take some of your power away. This section tells you about some of the problems kings faced and what happened. These are:

- problems with the Church leading to the murder of Thomas Becket
- problems with the BARONS leading to the siege of Kenilworth Castle
- problems with the peasants leading to the Peasants' Revolt.

SECTION 2
THE NORMAN CONQUEST

A turning point!
On a grassy hill in southern England a decisive battle has reached a decisive moment. The winner will rule England, and the country will never be the same again.

In this section you are going to try to work out why a Norman army was invading England, why they won, and how this conquest affected ordinary people in England.

England in the 1060s

▶▶ **William, Duke of Normandy, is thinking of invading England. On pages 8–9 you are going to be a spy for the Normans to find out if England was a strong country in 1066.**

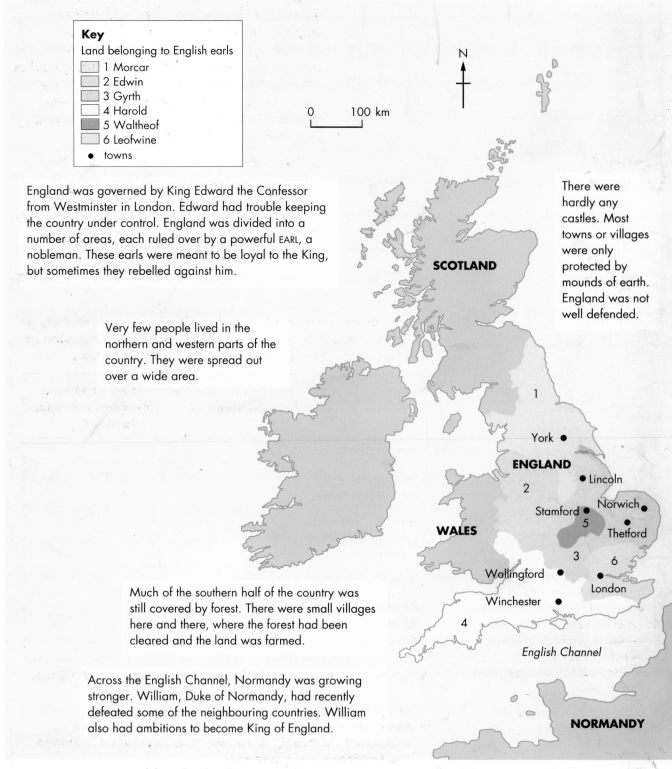

Key

Land belonging to English earls

- 1 Morcar
- 2 Edwin
- 3 Gyrth
- 4 Harold
- 5 Waltheof
- 6 Leofwine
- • towns

0   100 km

England was governed by King Edward the Confessor from Westminster in London. Edward had trouble keeping the country under control. England was divided into a number of areas, each ruled over by a powerful EARL, a nobleman. These earls were meant to be loyal to the King, but sometimes they rebelled against him.

Very few people lived in the northern and western parts of the country. They were spread out over a wide area.

There were hardly any castles. Most towns or villages were only protected by mounds of earth. England was not well defended.

Much of the southern half of the country was still covered by forest. There were small villages here and there, where the forest had been cleared and the land was farmed.

Across the English Channel, Normandy was growing stronger. William, Duke of Normandy, had recently defeated some of the neighbouring countries. William also had ambitions to become King of England.

▲ **SOURCE 1** *A map of England in the 1060s showing major towns and earldoms (areas ruled by an earl)*

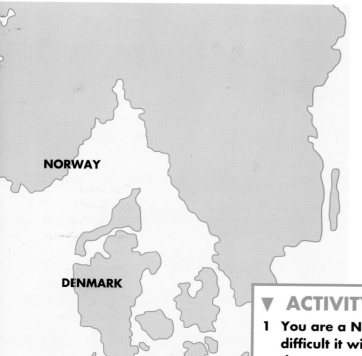

NORWAY

DENMARK

▼ **SOURCE 2** *Descriptions of the English and the Normans in the 1060s written by William of Malmesbury, a monk. He was half English and half Norman by birth*

a) The English, at that time, wore short garments reaching to the midknee; they had their hair cropped; their beards shaven; their arms covered with golden bracelets; their skins covered with punctured designs. Drinking parties were very common and they drank until they were sick. Drunkenness weakens the human mind and they often fought with rashness and fury rather than with military skill.

b) The Normans were very particular in their dress and ate and drank with care and not to excess. They were used to war, and could hardly live without it. They were fierce in rushing against the enemy, and where strength failed they tricked and deceived the enemy.

The English army consisted of:

■ around 3000 'housecarls', tough soldiers who fought with double-bladed axes which could split a man in half

■ earls in command of the mainly untrained peasants they brought with them from their villages

■ soldiers paid by townspeople to fight for them.

It was a good fighting force but difficult to gather together.

▼ ACTIVITY

1 **You are a Norman spy sent by William to see how easy or difficult it will be to INVADE England. Use the information on these pages to complete a copy of the table below.**

	What have you discovered?	Would this make it easier or harder to invade?
Are the defences good?		
How are people spread out over the country?		
Does the King have good control over England?		
Is the army strong?		
Are the English better fighters than the Normans?		

2 **Write a short report for William telling him your findings.**

▼ DISCUSS

3 **Read Source 2 again. How reliable is this source as evidence? Do you think the monk who wrote it favoured the English or the Normans?**

From across the water

▶▶ **William did decide to invade. Pages 10–11 tell you about the Normans landing in England.**

The date is 27 September 1066, early in the morning. The place, Pevensey, on the south coast of England. A boy and a girl head for the ruins of the old Roman fort on the cliffs. They have a hunk of black bread soaked in warm milk to eat for breakfast as they watch the sun come up over the sea. They have already milked the cow and done their chores around the farmhouse.

From where they sit, they have a good view of the beach and the sea beyond. As they look out on the cold, crisp morning they shiver in the light breeze coming off the water. The girl suddenly points out to sea. Some dark shapes are beginning to form on the horizon and they seem to be coming towards the beach. As the shapes get closer the children see that they are ships – many ships.

They watch the ships come closer and closer until they land on the beach below. The children watch nervously …

▼ ACTIVITY

1 a) Match the captions below to the pictures in Sources 1–3.

> **Captions**
> The Norman army lands
> The Normans prepare a feast
> The Norman fleet approaches the coast of England

b) Put the pictures in the correct order.

2 Look at Source 1:

- how are the two cooks (A) cooking the meat
- what are the men at (B) doing
- what is happening at (C)?

3 You are the girl or the boy. Tell the people in the village what you have seen. Give them detailed information about the ships, the soldiers' clothing, their weapons and what they have brought with them? How well prepared do you think the Normans are? Write down or role play what you might say.

▼ **SOURCE 3**

▲ SOURCE 1

▲ SOURCE 2

Sources 1–3 come from the Bayeux Tapestry. It was embroidered in the 1070s to tell the story of their invasion of England

Who should be the King of England?

On 5 January 1066, King Edward the Confessor died. He had no children so there was no one who would naturally become the next King of England. Three men now claimed to be the rightful king. They all had a good claim. But which one had the best claim? Pages 12–13 will help you find out.

▼ **SOURCE 1** *The three people who thought they should be King of England*

Harold Godwineson

My family are the most powerful in England. We have controlled Wessex for years. We intend to control all England one day.

Fifteen years ago we tried to take over. We rebelled and tried to get rid of King Edward the Confessor. But he beat us and threw us out of England.

But I came back. I wasn't going to be beaten that easily.

I have the best claim to the throne. I'm related to Edward – he is my brother-in-law. I am the only Englishman. And – note this very carefully – on his death-bed Edward said 'I commend all the kingdom to your protection.' **Edward wanted me to be king**! What more can I tell you?

By the way, don't confuse me with the other Harald (spelt differently and smells different too – what a cheek to think a Viking could be King of England).

Also don't believe what William says about oaths. Whatever I said, I was forced.

William, Duke of Normandy

I am a patient man. Fifteen years ago I was promised the throne of England when Edward died. Now I am ready to take it.

You wonder how this came about. Let me tell you. Edward loved us Normans. He grew up with us here in Normandy from when he was a boy until when he became King of England in 1042. It was only natural for him to call for my help when he faced a rebellion in 1051 (from that disloyal Harold Godwineson). I sent my best soldiers to help Edward. In return **Edward promised me I would be king when he died**.

Oh and another thing, last year Harold also needed my help. I was holding his nephew prisoner here and Harold came to release him. 'On one condition' I said. 'Edward promised me I would be king when he dies. If you support me in that, I will let you have your nephew back.' And Harold swore loyalty to me. So there you are . . . I should be king.

Harald Hardraada

It's Harald, with two 'a's. Don't mix me up with that Wessex Harold. I'm a Viking. I'm King of Norway.

Why should I be King of England? Well the North of England is ruled by Vikings – has been for one and a half centuries – and England has had loads of Viking kings. From 1016–1042 **they were all Vikings** – until that Edward seized the throne from us rightful kings.

Now that Edward has died England should have a Viking king again. If I'm not given the crown I will take it by force. I have an army ready to invade. The people in the North of England will support me in this. I'll be unbeatable.

| **King Cnut** |
| King of England from 1016–1035 (also King of Denmark and Norway). Passed on his throne to his son |

↓

| **King Harthacnut** |
| King of England 1040–42. Lost the throne but claimed he was the rightful king of England and promised the throne to |

↓

| **King Magnus of Norway** |
| who passed on the claim to the next king of Norway |

↓

| **Harald Hardraada** |

▲ **SOURCE 2** *Harald Hardraada's claim to the English throne*

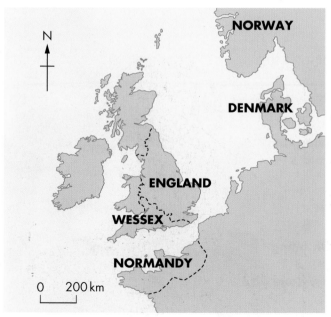

▲ **SOURCE 3** *A map of England (including Wessex), Norway, Denmark and Normandy*

▼ ACTIVITY

1 **Make a copy of the chart below. As you complete column 2 think about:**
a) **whether Edward wanted this person to be king**
b) **was he related to any previous King of England**
c) **was he from the right country**
d) **had he been promised the throne by anyone?**

Person	Why he thought he should be King of England
Harold Godwineson	
William of Normandy	
Harald Hardraada	

2 **Now divide into small groups for a class debate. Each group will support one claimant. Use what you have learnt on pages 12–13 to:**

a) **put the case for your claimant**
b) **say why the other two claimants should not be king.**

Why did William win the Battle of Hastings?

▶▶ In 1066 England was invaded twice. There were two bloody battles for the English throne and England had three kings. From this year of crisis William of Normandy emerged as the winner. Over the next eight pages you are going to examine why William won. Was he the best prepared? Was he the best leader? Or was he just the luckiest? At the end of this enquiry you will be writing an essay to explain in your own words why William won.

THE MONTHS BEFORE THE BATTLE

Harold Godwineson becomes king

Harold Godwineson did not wait to see what William or Harald Hardraada would do. He had an advantage over the others – he was **in England**, the others were abroad. So as soon as Edward died Harold went to London and had himself secretly crowned king.

He knew William and Harald would not back down. He knew he would have to fight them at some point. So all through the summer he got his army ready. The big question was who would he have to fight first?

What should Harold do?

Think hard about Harold's situation. Source 1 shows you his situation in the summer of 1066. There were two armies ready to invade – one to the north, one to the south. Harold could:

- guard the south coast
- guard the north coast
- split his forces and guard both coasts
- ignore both invading armies and get on with being king.

▼ SOURCE 1 *Threats to Harold in 1066*

> **I** have 5000 well-armed soldiers in London. I can get them to the north coast in ten days, or to the south coast in three days. But I'm really not sure which to do.

> **William's** army is ready. I've been told he has 5000 foot soldiers and 2000 knights on horseback. People are also saying he has a fleet of ships to carry his forces across the channel. Luckily for me the wind is blowing in the wrong direction, but he could invade at any moment if the wind changes.

▼ **ACTIVITY**

1 Working with a partner, draw up a table showing the advantages and disadvantages of each of Harold's options. These were:
   a) guard the south coast
   b) guard the north coast
   c) split his forces and guard both coasts
   d) ignore both invading armies and get on with being king.
   If you can think of something else he could have done add it to your table.

2 Now look at what Harold did (on the opposite page). Did he choose well?

What should I do?

People say that **Harald** is preparing an invasion fleet of around 500 ships and possibly 10,000 men. He'll probably get support from the King of Scotland and from Viking families in the north of England. He's also got the support of my very own brother, Tosti.

What did Harold do?

Harold decided to wait with his army on the south coast. He thought that William presented the greatest danger. But the weather meant William stayed in Normandy. At the end of the summer Harold sent his army home because he could not continue to feed them.

Harold beats the Norwegians

Just after he had done this, Harald Hardraada, with his fleet of 500 ships, swept into the River Tyne in the north-east. On 20 September his Norwegian army landed and fought the English Earls Edwin and Morcar. After a long fight, the English fled.

Harold was now in a desperate position. He had to gather his army together again and march hundreds of miles north to fight the Norwegians. On 25 September he met them at Stamford Bridge. It was a bloody battle in which Harald Hardraada was killed. His army was beaten. Most of his ships were burnt. Only 24 returned to Norway.

Bad news!

Harold had won a great victory but only three days later he received shattering news – William's invasion force had landed in the south! The wind direction had changed and William's fleet had been able to make the crossing. He had waited patiently until the time was right and luck was on his side – Harold was stuck in the north.

Just think how Harold must have felt! Now he had to get his army, or what was left of it, back to the south as quickly as he could. They would be very tired. On the other hand, he was a powerful warrior, feeling good about his victory over the Norwegians. On the following page you can see what happened next.

WHY DID WILLIAM WIN THE BATTLE OF HASTINGS?

THE WEEKS BEFORE THE BATTLE

▼ ACTIVITY

1 Working in pairs, discuss the events on the timeline below and study Sources 2–5. Who do you think is going to be best prepared for the battle – Harold or William?
   Use the table below to help you decide. Add as much information as possible under the headings in each column. Two examples have been done for you. You may find that some columns are more full than others.

2 Complete this sentence giving at least three reasons:

   We are backing . . . to win the battle. We think this because . . .

William		Harold	
Well prepared because ...	Not well prepared because ...	Well prepared because ...	Not well prepared because ...
he had a great host of fresh soldiers, horsemen and archers		he had just won a great battle – this gave Harold and his men a lot of confidence	

Harold

William

MOVEMENTS IN THE WEEKS LEADING UP TO THE BATTLE

1066

Harold wins a great victory against the Norwegians at Stamford Bridge	Sept 25	
	Sept 27	The wind changes direction and William's fleet leaves France
	Sept 28	William's fleet lands early in the morning
	Sept 29	William's forces occupy Hastings, preparing for battle
Harold marches south (covering 50 miles [80 kilometres] a day), leaving many of his archers in the north	Oct 2	
Harold reaches London and gathers together a new army, mainly made up of foot-soldiers	Oct 6	
Harold leaves London and marches 58 miles (93 kilometres) to Hastings	Oct 11	
Harold arrives at Hastings during the night, with an army of 7000 exhausted men	Oct 13	
	Oct 14	

THE BATTLE OF HASTINGS

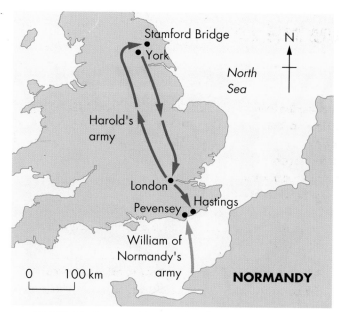

▲ **SOURCE 2** *Harold's and William's movements*

▼ **SOURCE 3** *Written in about 1115 by Florence of Worcester, a monk*

Harold marched his army towards London by forced marches; and, although he knew that he had lost some of his best men in the recent battle, and that half of his troops were not yet assembled, he did not hesitate to meet the enemy.

William, Count of the Normans, had arrived with a countless host of horsemen, slingers, archers and foot-soldiers, and had brought with him also powerful help from all parts of France.

▲ **SOURCE 4** *The Normans having time to relax before the battle*

▲ **SOURCE 5** *The Norman cavalry ready for battle*

WHY DID WILLIAM WIN THE BATTLE OF HASTINGS?

THE DAY OF THE BATTLE

It is October 14, and a misty morning. Two armies face each other on a shallow hillside near Hastings. What will happen next?

▲ **SOURCE 6** *A scene from the Bayeux Tapestry*

▼ **SOURCE 7** *A Norman account by William of Poitiers. He was not at the battle*

William's army advanced steadily in good order. The crossbowmen were at the front. Next came the infantry, and the KNIGHTS were at the back.

Harold's army was a vast host, gathered from all the provinces of England and reinforced by their allies the Danes. They did not care to fight on equal terms, so they took up their position on a hill with the forest behind them. They dismounted and drew themselves up in close order on foot.

The Norman foot-soldiers then attacked, but it seemed they would be overwhelmed by the English missiles. Then our knights crashed into the enemy with their shields. The English remained on high ground and kept close order. They were superior in numbers and in the way their spears broke our shields. Thus they pushed our knights down the hill.

William stood out boldly in front of those in flight, and restored their courage. Our men marched up the hill a second time. They realised that they would suffer heavy losses, but then remembered the trick of retreating. They turned round and pretended to flee. Several thousand English quickly gave pursuit. The Normans suddenly turned their horses, surrounded the enemy and cut them down. Twice this trick was used with great success.

▼ **SOURCE 8** *An English account from the ANGLO-SAXON Chronicle*

William took Harold by surprise before his men were ready for battle. The English army had a very small space; and many soldiers, seeing the difficult position, deserted King Harold. Even so, he fought bravely from dawn to dusk, and the enemy's army made little impression on him until, after a great slaughter on both sides, the King fell.

▼ **ACTIVITY**

1 The cartoons on page 19 show scenes from the battle. Which of the cartoons matches Source 6?
2 Use Source 7 to put the cartoons on page 19 in the correct order.
3 How do the cartoons and sources show that:
   a) William was a brave and courageous leader
   b) the Normans played a clever trick on the English?
4 Were there any moments when Harold could have won the battle?

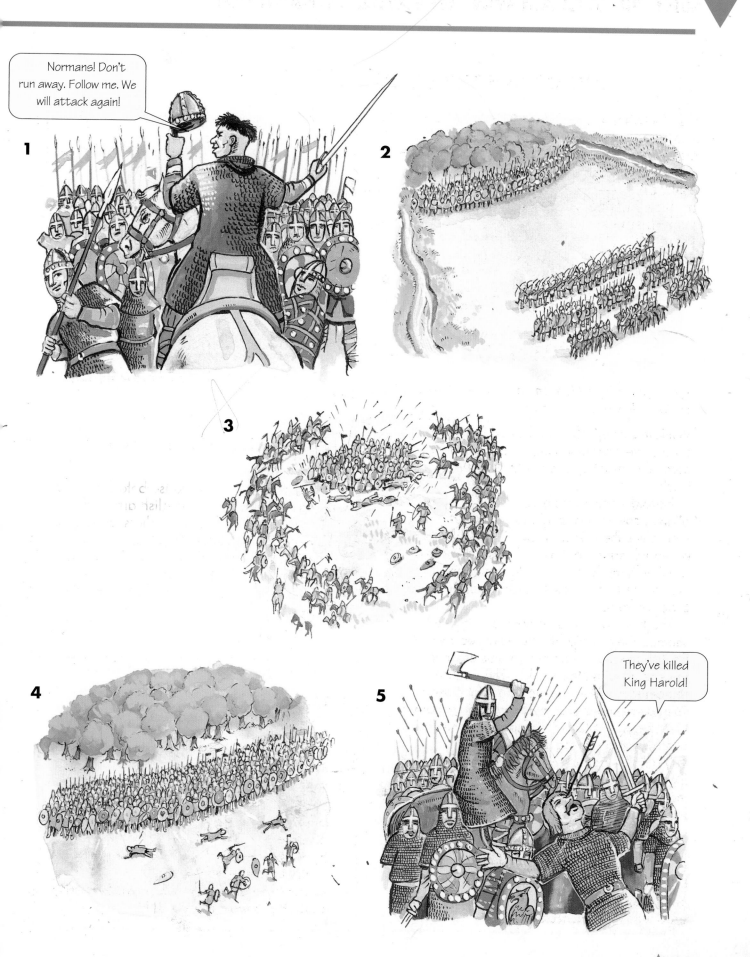

WHY DID WILLIAM WIN THE BATTLE OF HASTINGS?

▼ ACTIVITY

Over the last few pages you have gathered a lot of information about the reasons why William won the Battle of Hastings. Now you are going to put all this together to write an essay.

Organising your information

When you think back through your work, you will remember information about the following:

- preparations – how well prepared William was for the invasion
- leadership – William's skill and courage as a leader
- luck – how unlucky Harold was and how lucky William was.

Write the headings on a piece of paper as shown below.

Preparations	Leadership	Luck

Now look at statements 1–10. Put these statements under the correct headings. For example: statement 6 goes under the 'Preparations' heading.

1 William was very brave. At a difficult time in the battle he led his men back up the hill to attack the English.

2 At a key moment in the battle, Harold was killed.

3 William encouraged his men to use the clever trick of retreating to make the English come down from the hill. Then the Normans could surround and kill them.

6 William had assembled a great army and a great store of weapons.

7 Harold's men were exhausted by the time they got to Hastings and were not ready for the battle.

8 William had built many ships to carry his forces across the sea.

Writing your essay

Use the statements to write a paragraph about each of the areas – preparations, leadership and luck. You can use this writing frame to get started.

You might have some ideas about other points to add. For instance, you might think that Harold made some mistakes:

- perhaps he should have waited for all his troops to arrive, particularly the archers
- he may have made the journey too quickly
- possibly he should have rested his troops before the battle.

If you agree with any of these, or if you have other ideas about Harold's mistakes, add them in under another paragraph starting 'Harold also made some mistakes . . .'.

Why did William win the Battle of Hastings?

William, Duke of Normandy, won the Battle of Hastings in 1066. In this essay I am going to give some of the main reasons why he won.

One of the reasons William won was because he had made good preparations. He . . .

Another reason was that he was a brave and skilful leader. He . . .

William was also much luckier than Harold. He . . .

---

4 The wind had changed at the right time for William. He was able to cross the sea and land in Hastings while Harold was still fighting in the north.

5 Some of Harold's best soldiers had been killed fighting the Norwegians in the north.

9 William had a large force of knights on horses (cavalry) which gave the Normans a lot of attacking power.

10 William skilfully arranged his army in rows – archers, foot-soldiers and cavalry – for the attack.

How did William gain control of England?

▶▶ **William has won the Battle of Hastings. But there is a big difference between winning a battle and gaining a country. On pages 22–25 you are now going to investigate how he gained control of the rest of England.**

▼ **SOURCE 1** *A map of England showing the threats to William*

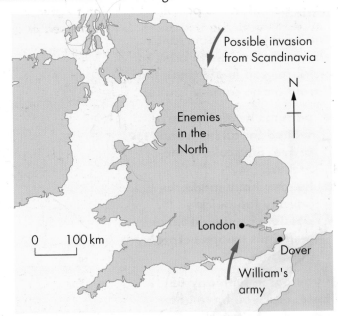

▼ **ACTIVITY A**

William's problems

Put yourself in William's position after the Battle of Hastings. You have defeated Harold but you have only conquered a small corner of the country. There is a lot more to do and many problems to face. Some of the problems are shown in Sources 1 and 2.

Decide:
a) which problems need to be dealt with straight away (short-term problems) and which can wait till later
b) the order in which you will deal with these short-term problems
c) how you can deal with the short-term problems.

5 Many of the English lords do not want to accept me as king. I cannot trust them to keep their parts of the country under control. I need to find a way of keeping the whole country under control.

1 There is still a threat of invasion from Scandinavia, supported by rebellion in the north of England. I have many enemies in the north. I must bring these people under control.

2 London is England's capital city. I must take control of it quickly. Some of Harold's troops, who did not come with him to Hastings, are still in London and could cause problems for me.

4 I need to collect taxes, but I do not know how much wealth there is in the country and who owns what.

3 There is a very strong castle full of English soldiers in Dover. If things go wrong for me they could cut off my route back to Normandy.

▲ **SOURCE 2** *Some of the problems William faced in 1066*

▼ ACTIVITY B

William's solutions

You are William. Use Sources 3–5 below and Source 6 on page 25 to describe how you:

- **solved the problem in Dover**
- **persuaded the people of London to give in**
- **dealt with the trouble in the north (see pages 24–25).**

▲ **SOURCE 3** *Norman soldiers attacking Englishmen. A picture from a medieval* MANUSCRIPT

▼ **SOURCE 4** *Written by William of Poitiers in around 1071. He fought for William of Normandy*

Then William marched to Dover, which was held by a large force. The English were stricken with fear and prepared to surrender unconditionally, but our men, greedy for booty, set fire to the castle and the greater part of it was destroyed. The Duke, unwilling that those who had offered to surrender should suffer loss, gave them money for the damage. Having taken possession of the castle, the Duke spent eight days adding new fortifications to it.

▼ **SOURCE 5** *Florence of Worcester describing William's movements before he went to London*

Earl William was laying waste Sussex, Kent, Hampshire, Surrey, Middlesex and Hertfordshire and ceased not from burning villages and slaughtering the inhabitants. He was then met by the Earls Edwin and Morcar and Londoners of the better sort, who submitted to him.

▼ **SOURCE 6** *Written about 60 years after the events described, by a monk trained in Normandy. He describes how William dealt with his enemies in the north of England*

The royal forces approached York, only to learn that the Danes had fled. The King ordered his men to comb forests and remote mountainous places, stopping at nothing to hunt out the enemy hidden there. He cut down many in his vengeance; destroyed the lairs of others; harried the land; and burned homes to ashes. Nowhere else had William shown such cruelty. He made no effort to control his fury and punished the innocent with the guilty. In his anger he ordered that all crops, herds and food of every kind should be brought together and burned to ashes, so that the whole region north of the Humber might be stripped of all means of sustenance. As a result of this such a terrible famine fell upon the humble and defenceless people that more than 100,000 Christian folk of both sexes, young and old alike, perished of hunger.

▼ ACTIVITY

1 **You are an English lord who is resisting William in the north of England. You make a speech to persuade people to join you. Use the ideas below if you wish.**

My loyal friends,

I come to ask for your help against the tyrant, William. Just look what he has done to our people. He has laid waste and destroyed our land.

He has burnt …

He brutally hunted down …

He took all their …

The result of this is that …

We can stand this no longer. I call on you to …

You might be scared because …

But you must resist because …

▼ THE OTHER SIDE

2 **Wouldn't it be nice if all characters in history gave a neat explanation for their actions? Write one paragraph for William to explain why he was so brutal.**

How did William keep control?

▶▶ **It took William several years but eventually he put down all the rebellions against him. However, he still had some long term problems which he needed to solve to stay in control. On pages 26–29 you are going to investigate how he solved these problems.**

▼ ACTIVITY

Divide a page of your book into two columns, as below. Fill in these columns as you read this section. In the left-hand column, explain each problem briefly using William's thought bubbles below (one has been done for you). In the right-hand column, say briefly how he solved it using the 'solution' boxes on pages 27–28. Be careful – you will have one of William's problems left over.

Problem	How William solved it
Rewarding his followers and keeping them loyal	

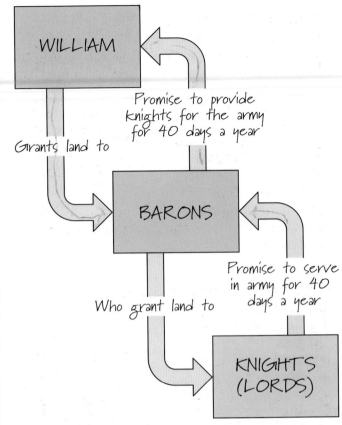

▲ **SOURCE 1** *How William granted land in return for service in his army*

Problems

A. I must reward the people who have helped me conquer England and make sure they stay loyal to me in the future. How do I do this?

B. How can I make sure the English obey my laws?

C. What's the best way to keep the English under control and stop them attacking my soldiers?

D. I need to have an army ready to fight off any attacks but I can't afford to pay for this day after day.

E. I need more money to pay for all sorts of things: for the army, for great buildings and for my rich lifestyle – after all I am a king! The problem is I do not know how wealthy they are. How can I get money out of the English when I don't know what they own?

Solution 1: Grant land

I took most of the land from the English landowners and gave it to Norman barons (powerful lords) who were loyal to me. I gave my brother Odo around 400 ESTATES. The barons could not run all the estates so they shared out their land with the knights who fought with them during the conquest of England.

Solution 3: Appoint sheriffs

I made some of my barons into SHERIFFS. Their job is to collect my taxes and keep law and order. I understand that some of the sheriffs have been hard on the English but I don't care. The English people must obey my laws. Some people have said that England is a safer place now because of my strict laws.

Solution 2: Demand soldiers

In return for the land I gave them, I made the barons promise to send me knights for 40 days each year. If I work this out carefully, I will always have an army of nearly 4000 men in case anybody attacks me.

Solution 4: Collect information

I sent out my officials all over the country – to every village – to collect information about what people owned. The English didn't like it and there were some riots. But I told them I would kill anybody who was not honest about what they owned.

How much land does the manor have?

Answer: 10 hides (=1200 acres)

What is the manor called?

Answer:

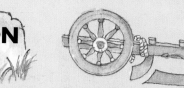

How many ploughs were there?

Answer: The Lord has 4 ploughs. The villagers have 20 ploughs.

How many mills are there?

How much meadow is there?

Answer: 170 acres

Answer: 2 mills

How many villagers are there?

Answer: 28 villagers and a priest

▲ **SOURCE 2** *William's officials went to over 13,000 villages. This source shows the questions asked and the answers given in the village of Elton in Cambridgeshire. All the information was written down in a great book called the* **Domesday Book**

Solution 5: Build castles

Oh yes, I nearly forgot – castles! Castles were one of **the main reasons** we were able to control the English. We built castles throughout the country. At the start these were just wooden castles on mounds of earth like the one in Source 3. It only took us two or three weeks to build each one. Later, when we had more time, we turned some of these into stone castles, which were much stronger.

Castles provided protection for my soldiers. The English found it almost impossible to capture castles. Also, we used castles as bases. One Norman baron and his soldiers could control quite a large area of countryside around his castle. About fifty soldiers in a castle could hold off an army of thousands of English.

▲ **SOURCE 3** *The early castles William built were called motte and bailey castles. The motte was a large mound with a wooden tower on top of it. The bailey was a large fenced area surrounding the motte. This is a modern drawing of the building of the motte and bailey castle at Pickering in Yorkshire*

▲ SOURCE 4

▼ **ACTIVITY**

Use Sources 3 and 4 to draw and label your own diagram of a motte and bailey castle. Add notes to your diagram, with arrows pointing to key parts of the castle, to explain why it was difficult to attack.

◄ **SOURCE 5** *A map showing the castles built in England and Wales by the end of William's reign. Some castles were in the middle of the countryside. A few were in towns. In Lincoln 166 houses were destroyed to make way for the new castle. The castles guarded roads, rivers, bridges – any possible invasion route*

Key
Highland
Castle

N

0   100 km

Review: The Norman Conquest

▼ REVIEW ACTIVITY

Remember the children who witnessed the Norman landing in 1066 (see page 10)? It is now 1087, the year of William the Conqueror's death. They were separated after the Battle of Hastings. Now they meet again and tell each other what has happened to them and what they have seen. Tell one of their stories.

The boy

He fled with some other villagers running away from William's army, as it laid waste to the countryside. He ended up in the north and saw the way William put down the rebellion there. He was forced into helping to build a motte and bailey castle which was later attacked. He lived and worked in the village nearby which was kept under strict Norman control. After years of this he escaped and came home. Tell his story. Include in it:

- what happened to him after he left
- what he saw in the north
- what he and the other villagers had to do to build the motte and bailey castle
- what happened when the castle was attacked
- why he hated the Normans so much.

The girl

She stayed in the village. Life soon settled down and was much the same as before. A motte and bailey castle was built nearby and the land and the village became part of a Norman lord's estate. The Normans brought law and order and life was very safe. Later the village got a new stone church. Include in the girl's story:

- the arrival of the Norman lord, Roger Bigod, and his soldiers, to claim control of the village as part of his estate
- the building of a motte and bailey castle nearby (which was later turned into a stone castle)
- the coming of the Domesday inspectors and what questions they asked
- how safe life was
- why she liked the Normans.

SECTION 3
LIVING IN MEDIEVAL TIMES

A peasant's life!

Nine out of ten people in the Middle Ages were peasants. They lived, worked and died in the same tiny villages around the country. Mostly they farmed. They sowed, weeded, harvested, and the following year they sowed, weeded and harvested again, and on it went year after year.

Was theirs a good life? Would you have liked it?
What was it really like to live in medieval times?
How hard was it? What dangers were there?
How did they cope with disasters?
What did they hope for in the next world?

These are some of the questions you will think about as you investigate what life was like in medieval villages.

It's a hard life being a peasant!

How do we know what medieval villages looked like?

▶▶ **Most medieval villages crumbled away a long time ago. So how do we find out what they looked like? Pages 32–39 reveal all.**

Nearly everybody in the Middle Ages lived in the countryside. There were small clusters of houses here and there, with sometimes a hundred, sometimes several hundred people living in them. These villages, with the land around them, were called manors and were held and controlled by a lord of the manor.

What did these villages look like?

The village of Wharram Percy in Yorkshire

The first village we are going to look at, Wharram Percy, no longer exists. Apart from the church, there are no buildings left, just fields. But because the land has not been built on by later generations, there are many remains for ARCHAEOLOGISTS to excavate.

◀ **SOURCE 1**
A photograph of Wharram Percy from the air. Photographs like this were taken for the first time in the 1940s. They can show details of what is just below the surface of the ground

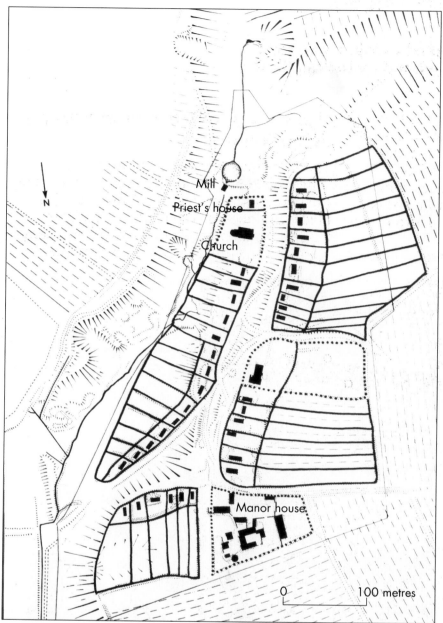

Mill
Priest's house
Church

Manor house

0   100 metres

▲ **SOURCE 2** *The archaeologists were eventually able to produce this plan of Wharram Percy*

Wharram Percy, like some other medieval villages, was deserted by 1500. Until the 1940s, almost everyone had forgotten that there ever was a village called Wharram Percy. After the villagers left, the houses fell down and grass grew over the foundations and pathways. But over the last 50 years, using evidence such as Sources 1 and 3, archaeologists have been able to discover what it was like.

▼ **SOURCE 3** *Evidence noticed by archaeologists*

- A parish church stands isolated in the middle of fields.
- Three fields close to the church are called 'Water Lane', 'Towngate' and 'Town Street'.
- There are stone foundations of rows of rectangular houses.

▼ DISCUSS

How were the archaeologists able to draw the plan of Wharram Percy in Source 2? Use Sources 1 and 3 to help you. How do you think they worked out:

a) where the roads were?
b) where the edges of the fields were?

c) which were the villagers' houses?
d) which building was the manor house where the lord of the manor lived?
e) where the church was?
f) that there was a mill and a mill pond next to the church?

HOW DO WE KNOW WHAT MEDIEVAL VILLAGES LOOKED LIKE?

A reconstruction of Wharram Percy

In Source 4 you can see a reconstruction of Wharram Percy. This has been done by an artist who has been given very specific information about what the village might have looked like and the positions of the houses, roads, church and so on.

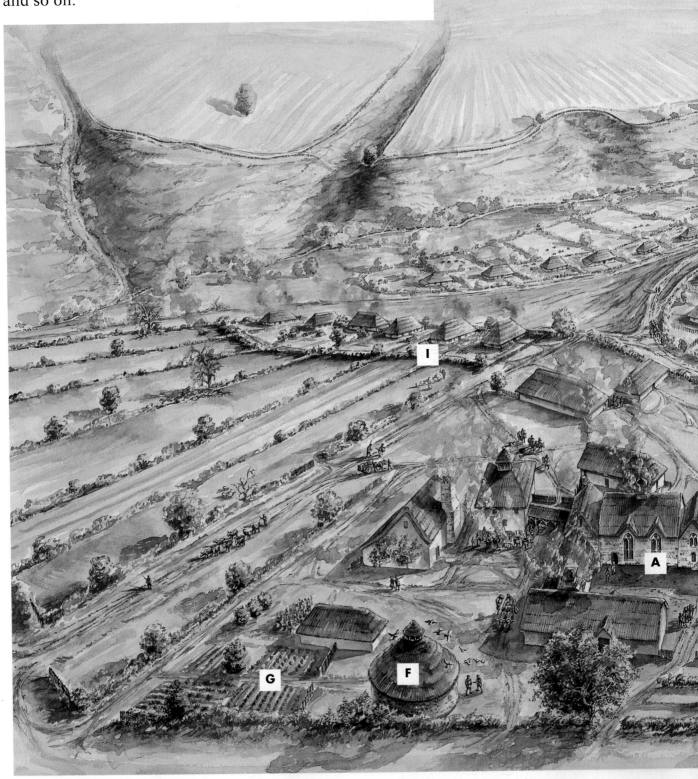

◄ **SOURCE 4** *A reconstruction of what Wharram Percy probably looked like in the Middle Ages*

▼ **ACTIVITY**

1 **Match the letters on the drawing with the items in this list:**

- barn
- manor house
- church
- dovecote
- villager's house
- animals grazing
- mill
- kitchen garden for the manor house
- wagon.

2 **There are some things in the drawing which could not be worked out from the archaeological evidence.**
a) **Can you find them?**
b) **What kind of evidence do you think was used to find out these details?**

3 **Using Sources 1–4, write a description of the village as it was during the Middle Ages. A few ideas to start you off are set out below.**

A main road ran down the centre of the village. Along it were . . .

The manor house was separated from the peasants' houses. This was the largest . . .

There were buildings around the manor house. For example . . .

▶▶ **You are now going to see how written and pictorial evidence can help us find out about medieval villages.**

The village of Elton in Cambridgeshire

Much of the evidence you will use in this section is about the village of Elton. Unlike Wharram Percy, Elton is still a thriving village today. All the medieval buildings were destroyed long ago and archaeologists have not been able to excavate the ruins. Yet we can still work out what life in Elton was like, even if we can't find out everything we would like to know.

For a start there is the Domesday Book (see page 27). Every village in England was described there, so sure enough there is an entry for Elton.

▼ **SOURCE 5** *From the Domesday Book, the survey William ordered to find out what everybody owned*

In Elton the Abbot of Ramsey had 10 hides of land. There are now 4 ploughs on the DEMESNE. There are 28 villeins having 20 ploughs. There is a church and a priest, and 2 mills with an income of 40s a year. There are 170 acres [69 hectares] of meadow.

Note on money
Before decimal coins were introduced in 1971, there were pennies, shillings and pounds:
12d (old pennies) made a shilling
20s (shillings) made a pound.

▼ **SOURCE 6** *From another royal survey 100 years after the Domesday Book*

2 water mills and a fulling mill also belonged to the Abbot; also fishing rights on the river.

The manor of Elton belonged to the Abbot of Ramsey Abbey, who also held 23 other manors. He did not live in Elton and rarely visited it. His officials ran the manor for him. They had to keep records such as Sources 7 and 13 of all the money spent and received.

▼ **SOURCE 7** *Examples from the thirteenth-century records of money spent by the lord*

1286 6d paid for branches for the barn and the sheepfold.
1297 12d paid for the hiring of one ship for carrying 1200 bundles of rushes from Wytlesmare to Elton.
12d paid to a carpenter for work on the chapel 12 working days.
2s paid to a man thatching the barn during 32 days with board.
6d to a carpenter for making gates before the hall and barn during 6 days.
2d to a mason for repairing the walls before the great barn.
5s 2d for 4 men slating the chapel for 3 weeks.

These records tell us a lot about the buildings in Elton. Most of the evidence is about the buildings around the manor house, which belonged to the lord. Pictures from other villages can help us discover what these buildings in Elton might have looked like.

As well as these buildings there would have been dozens of peasant cottages. These would probably have been similar to the cottages in Source 4 on pages 34–35.

▲ SOURCE 8

▲ SOURCE 9

▼ **DISCUSS**

Which of the buildings shown in Sources 8–10 are mentioned in the written sources?

▲ **SOURCE 10** *This picture comes from the Luttrell Psalter – an illustrated prayer book*

► **SOURCE 11** *A barn*

▲ **SOURCE 12** *A manor house*

▼ **SOURCE 13** *Excerpts from the records of money paid to the lord of Elton*

1296 3s 4d rent from Adam Bird for a bread oven.

1307 6d from Robert the Smith for one smithy.

1350 40s rent for the 3 mills, 2 grist and 1 fulling.

▲ **SOURCE 14** *Baking bread in an oven*

ferrarij duo demul
cont ferrum

grella longa gest capire · Capur con

▲ **SOURCE 15** *A blacksmith's smithy*

▼ **SOURCE 16** *Examples taken from the fourteenth-century records of money spent by the lord of Elton*

1307 15d for a thatcher hired for 20 days to thatch the stable, the dovecote and the sheepfold.
4d for a mason to mend the wall between the manor house and the granary.

1311 9d paid to a mason for mending the dairy.

1313 2d paid to a carpenter for mending the common privy.
20d paid to two carpenters for mending the dovecote next to the chapel.

1324 16d paid to one slater for mending the roof of the manor house, kitchen and bakehouse during 16 days with food.

1345 3s 11d for stones and slates for making a new oven and furnace in the manor.

1350 12d for a mason for repairing the walls of the manor house after the flood.

▼ **ACTIVITY**

1 **Use Sources 5–16 to complete a copy of this table about the buildings in Elton. First find each different type of building and write it in the first column, then fill in the other columns. An example has been done for you.**

Type of building	What was it made of?	What was it used for?	Where was it?
sheepfold	branches and thatch	keeping the sheep in	near the manor house

2 **On a large copy of the outline map of Elton, which your teacher will give you, draw in the buildings where you think they would have been. Explain why you have put them in those particular places.**

▼ **DISCUSS**

3 **You have now used archaeological evidence to find out about Wharram Percy, and documentary evidence to find out about Elton. Which type of evidence was more useful?**

Living in a medieval village

You now know something about the buildings in a medieval village. On pages 40–47 you are going to find out what life was like for the people who lived in them. You are also going to find out how this all depended on whether you were a man or a woman, and whether you were rich or poor. You will use what you find to design and play a board game.

The lord of the manor owned all the land on a manor but he did not farm all of it. Most of the land was farmed by the villagers.

Most of the villagers can be divided into two groups: freemen and villeins.

Wife of another freeman

And what about the beer we brew? We can't sell it until the lord has decided on the price we can charge.

Freeman's wife

What about all the money we pay to the lord. We **have** to use his mill to grind our corn into flour and pay him for using it. If we use our own hand-mills, we get fined.

We can't bake bread in our houses. We **have** to use the lord's ovens and pay the bakers to bake our own bread … and they charge too much!

Freeman

We're supposed to be freemen but we have to do BOON-WORK for the lord when he wants us to – ploughing in spring or summer and, worst of all, helping to bring in his harvest when we should be collecting our own. We just want to farm our own land. Still … I suppose we are better off than the villeins.

■ **FREEMEN** paid rent to the lord to farm their land. In Elton in the twelfth century there were 22 freemen.

■ **VILLEINS** worked on the lord's land. In return they were given some land to farm for themselves. In Elton there were 48 villein

Villein

Why are you freemen complaining? We have to do all that you do and **more**. We only have a little plot of la for our own needs but when do we g a chance to work on it?

Think of all the things we have to d for the lord. We have to work for hi every week of the year – WEEK-WORK

That means at least one day's ploughing per week. All the other job weeding, mending fences, removin stones from fields and the like – ta another two days a week. And at harvest time he makes us work fi days a week, sometimes even mor

All the same things apply to us At least you are free to make yo own decisions. We have to ask hi permission to live outside the manor or if our daughters want get married. We have to pay him sum of money if our sons want t take over our land when we die. any of this fair?

Villein's wife

► **SOURCE 1** *Peasants being supervised by the bailiff at harvest time*

▲ **SOURCE 2** *Peasants making a rush fence for the lord's land in winter*

▼ ACTIVITY

1 **By modern standards the villeins' life was unfair. Complete this sentence by choosing one of the four alternatives and giving your reasons.**

   In my opinion the most unfair thing villeins had to do was . . .

   ■ **pay for bread to be baked in the lord's oven**
   ■ **work on the lord's land**
   ■ **pay money to the lord when a son or daughter took over the land**
   ■ **have to ask the lord's permission if their daughter wanted to get married**

   because . . .

2 **Would you rather have been a freeman or a villein? Write two or three sentences explaining your choice.**

LIVING IN A MEDIEVAL VILLAGE

The peasants' year

Men and women worked hard in medieval villages. Most of the time they worked side by side, although they also had separate jobs to do. Many of the jobs shown in Source 3 were done by both men and women.

In addition to these jobs there was other work that continued all year round – collecting firewood, digging drainage ditches, looking after animals, repairing houses and so on. Remember that as well as working on their own land villeins had to do their services for the lord. This could take up three to five days a week, or more at busy times like harvesting and hay-making.

▼ **SOURCE 3**

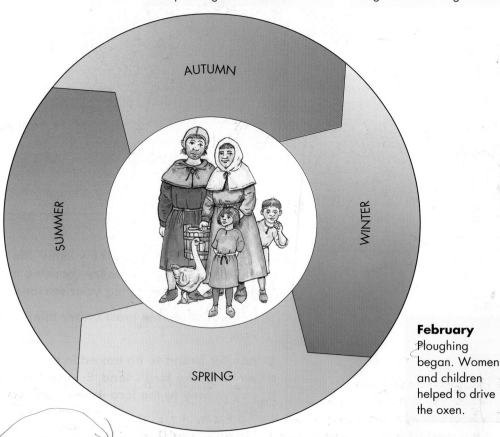

August and September
This was harvest time. All the family helped. The men would cut the crop with a scythe. The women tied the crop up in sheaves. The sheaves had to be carted from the field. Both the scything and the carting were dangerous jobs. The carts were loaded high and a fall could mean a broken neck.

The grain was then separated from its stalk and from the husks. This was called winnowing. The grain was usually stored in the lord's barn. The lord provided food and drink and gave all the workers a feast when the harvest was completed.

October
The field was sown with winter corn.

November
Some of the animals were butchered. The meat was salted and smoked so that it would keep through the winter.

January
Much time was spent on work around the house – getting firewood, planting vegetables in the garden.

February
Ploughing began. Women and children helped to drive the oxen.

July
Hemp and flax were gathered in by the women, and laid out to dry ready for spinning.

June
The sheep were sheared and the hay harvest in the meadow began. The hay was cut and then stacked in the barn. The cattle were allowed into the field to eat the stubble.

March
The seed for the oats and barley had to be sown. A harrow was then used to cover the seeds over with soil. Other jobs included weeding, chasing away birds and more ploughing.

▲ SOURCE 4

◀ SOURCE 5

◀ SOURCE 6

[top right image]

▲ SOURCE 7

▼ ACTIVITY

1 Study Sources 1, 2 and 4–7. Match each one with a month of the year explaining your choices.
2 Make up a board game about the peasants' year. If you are stuck your teacher can give you a model to follow. Include all the jobs and the services they might have to do. You can also invent some good and bad things that might happen, for example: 'You fall ill'; 'Your house catches fire'; 'A relative gives you a pig'. Two examples are shown opposite.

Lord insists that you do two extra days week-work for all of March to mend his fences. Go back two spaces.

A great harvest. All the food is gathered in. The lord of the manor is very pleased and puts on a big feast. Go forward five spaces.

LIVING IN A MEDIEVAL VILLAGE

Women in the village

It was normal for women to do some farm work every day. The cows had to be milked; the chickens, and usually a pig, had to be looked after. It was also very important to take care of the garden because it produced the family's vegetables. When their help was needed in the fields, women helped out doing the same jobs as men.

But they also had many other jobs to do, as you can see on these pages. Women did most of the household jobs. Before dawn the fire had to be lit.

Cleaning the house took little time. The houses were small and the floor was covered in straw. Even though chickens, pigs and other animals wandered in and out of the house, the women still tried to keep their houses clean. Archaeologists have found that many floors were swept so often that the brooms left U-shaped depressions.

▲ **SOURCE 8** *Other jobs for women included baking bread in the lord's ovens and taking grain to the mill. Women earned extra money by brewing beer – a very dangerous job, as it involved carrying twelve-gallon (55-litre) vats of hot liquid. Women also earned wages as thatchers and labourers*

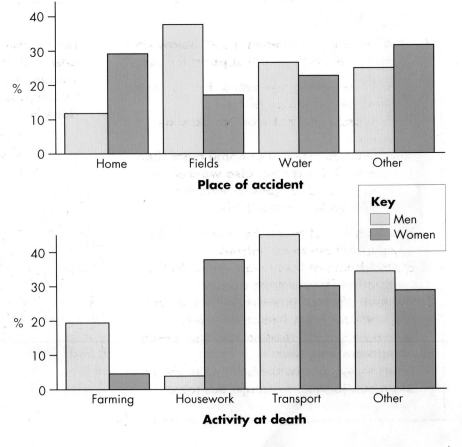

Place of accident

Key
Men
Women

► **SOURCE 9** *This information comes from the records of the Coroner's Courts in the fourteenth century. These courts investigated people's deaths. The first graph shows where in the village men and women died. The second shows what the men and women were doing when they died*

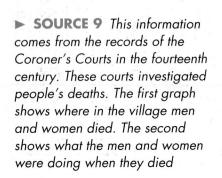

Activity at death

44 ▲

▲ **SOURCE 10** *Many women spun thread. They always carried their spindle with them so they could spin in between other jobs. The thread was sometimes made into rough cloth for the family, but more often it was sold to a weaver*

On top of all this, there were the children to look after. Babies were often wrapped in narrow bandages called swaddling clothes so they could not crawl around. Older babies were often tied into their cradles.

During busy times, when the women had to work in the fields they usually took them with them. The swaddled babies could be put in trees. Once a child was about five years old it would look after younger children.

▲ **SOURCE 11** *Water for cooking, washing and drinking had to be carried from the well to the house. Washing clothes was done by hand. It was a hard job*

▼ ACTIVITY

1 a) **Which one of statements A–C below do the figures in Source 9 support the most?**

  A Women only worked at home. They never helped in the fields.

  B Women did not work as hard as men.

  C Women worked at home more than men did, but they also worked at other kinds of jobs around the village and in the fields.

 b) **Which one of these statements do the figures show to be untrue?**

 c) **Which one of these statements do the figures tell us nothing about?**

2 **Using the figures in Source 9 and what you already know about the work women did, say whether you agree with this statement or not:**
'Women worked in the fields with the men, but they did the less dangerous jobs.'

3 **Look at the two people in the cartoon below. Write down how you think the woman might reply to the man. (She would probably tell him what she has done in the last two days.)**

> Of course, you women have a much easier life than us men.

The poor and the rich at home

Finding out about medieval life at home is a problem.

We have a lot more evidence about the homes of rich people than about poor people. For the rich there are written sources like letters, account books, paintings and family documents. Some of the houses of the rich have survived to the present day. But we do not have much evidence about the homes of the poor.

The reconstructions in Sources 12 and 13 are based on historical evidence about the homes of poor people and rich people but **not all houses would have been like these**.

▼ **DISCUSS**

Why do you think we do not have much evidence about the poor from:
a) things written by them or about them
b) their houses
c) their belongings?

▼ **SOURCE 12** *A poor person's house*

▼ ACTIVITY

Compare the homes of the poor and the rich in Sources 12 and 13. Use a table like the one started opposite. Add other rows to show things that would be helpful in making your comparison.

	Homes of the poor	Homes of the rich
Materials used to make the home		
Number of rooms		
Types of room		

▼ **SOURCE 13** *A rich person's house*

Could you get justice in the Middle Ages?

▶▶ Some people think that in the Middle Ages crimes were very violent and punishments very cruel. On pages 48–52 you will decide for yourself if that is really true.

The manorial court

The lord's manorial court was the court that ordinary people had most contact with (see Source 1). It was held several times a year, and everybody in the village had to attend or they would be fined.

The lord's steward was in charge of the court. It usually met in the hall of the manor house. In warm weather the court met outside.

The court heard two types of case:

- the lord's business – collecting money from the villagers and making sure they did the work they owed the lord
- sorting out arguments and keeping law and order in the village.

The jury

The JURY was made up of twelve villeins, chosen by the whole village. The jury collected all the evidence, presented it to the court and then decided whether defendants were guilty and how to punish them.

The hue and cry

This made sure everyone in the village helped to track down people who broke the law. For example, if a villager was attacked, he or she would raise the hue and cry. Everybody within earshot had to come to the rescue and help hunt for the guilty person. If the villagers did not help they were all fined!

Tithings

All men over the age of twelve were placed in groups of ten called tithings. Each member of the tithing had to make sure that the other members did not break the law. They often had to promise that they would pay a fine if another member committed a crime, or that he would behave himself in the future. If he did not, all the members of the tithing were fined.

▼ **SOURCE 1** *A manorial court*

a) Maud struck Emma and Emma raised the hue and cry upon her. And the hue and cry was not carried out.

b) John Joce let Peter, a stranger, stay at his house without the lord's permission.

c) Robert's oxen wandered onto the lord's land and damaged the barley growing there.

d) Alex, Gilbert and Henry badly beat Reynald.

e) John Lane assaulted Alice his stepmother in her own house and hit her with a stick, breaking her right hand.

f) Henry Godswein refused to work at the second boon-work of the autumn, and he ordered everyone to go home early.

g) Agnes, who is poor, gave birth to a child when she was not married.

h) Nicholas ploughed the lord's land very badly.

i) Robert owned a dog which ate a foal.

◀ **SOURCE 2** *A woman beating a man. An illustration from the Luttrell Psalter*

▼ ACTIVITY

1 **Look at the crimes listed in Source 3. What punishments do you think people received for these crimes? Some suggestions are listed below. Be careful – some of these punishments would not have been given and others may have been given more than once.**

List of punishments:

- made to pay a fine of 6d
- put in the stocks
- given a whipping
- hand cut off
- fined 2s
- whole village fined 2s
- no fine because the person was too poor
- fined 6d each and ordered to pay 1s damages.

2 **Which of these crimes would not be seen as crimes today? Explain why.**

3 **Your teacher will tell you which punishments were actually given. Which of the words in the box below would you use to describe the punishments:**

| fair | cruel | soft | unfair | tough |

cruel

▼ DISCUSS

4 **Why do you think everybody was required to help keep law and order? Do you think this idea should be used more today? Should the system of tithings be used in schools today?**

COULD YOU GET JUSTICE IN THE MIDDLE AGES?

Trial by ordeal – God decides

More serious crimes were dealt with in the King's courts. In the early Middle Ages, when juries could not agree about whether somebody was guilty or not, God could be asked to decide. The person who had been accused would have to undergo trial by ordeal. The trials were usually carried out in the church or as near to it as possible.

The method used for women was usually **trial by hot iron**. Here is what might have happened …

The story of Edith

Edith never married. At 38 she was past marrying age. She lived in a little cottage on the edge of the village. She grew her own vegetables on her own piece of land around the cottage. She kept a goat for milk. She got extra food and sometimes a little extra money from the other villagers because of her knowledge of herbs which could help cure their illnesses. She had learnt all this from her mother who had in turn learnt it from her mother before her.

One day she had been tending her vegetables when a group of villagers marched up.

'What did you give my husband?' cried Martha, a woman she knew well.

'Just some simple herbs to stop the pains in his stomach,' replied Edith. 'Why, what's wrong?'

'He's dead, that what's wrong,' replied Martha bitterly. 'You did it, you poisoned him, and you're going to be punished.'

Martha did not know what to say. She had scarce got her breath when she was grabbed by two of the men and dragged into the village. A few days later she was brought before the court but the jury could not agree whether she was guilty. Almost every member of the jury, or someone in their family, had at some time received herbs from her to relieve pain or cure rashes and sores.

'Let God decide,' shouted a villager and others agreed. Edith felt faint. She knew what this meant – the hot iron.

Edith had to fast (not eat anything) for three days. Then she had to hear mass

In the church a special area was set aside. Edith was given a piece of red-hot iron which she had to carry for three metres. Then her hand was bandaged

After three days the bandage was taken off and her as examined. Edith sobbe relief. Her wounds were not festering. Her hand was healing cleanly and she was judged innocent

50

One of the methods used for men was **trial by cold water.**

▼ **SOURCE 4**

It is said: 'Let this water be to thee now a trial.' The accused is undressed and cast, thumbs and toes tied together, into the water. And it is said: 'O thou water, in the name of God, do not receive this man if he be guilty, but make him swim upon thee.'

▼ **ACTIVITY**

The story of Richard

**Tell the story of Richard who undergoes trial by cold water.
Here is the beginning of your story.**

Richard is the village blacksmith. People are afraid of him. He is a loud man and his temper often gets him into trouble.

One frosty Sunday morning the village priest arrives at church to find the silver candlesticks missing from the altar. He calls out the hue and cry.

'I bet it was Richard the blacksmith who did it!' shouted one young man. 'I saw him running away from the church last night.'

The villagers run to Richard's house. He doesn't try to run away. They tie him up and search his room. They cannot find the candlesticks anywhere.

'I'm innocent' he booms. 'Untie me ...'

Still they don't believe him and a few weeks later he is in court on trial for his life. If he is guilty he will hang. But the jury can't decide. There is no evidence: no candlesticks, no-one actually saw him take them. But no-one trusts Richard.

'Let God show us if he is guilty' they say ...

What happens next? Complete this story by drawing two more pictures with captions to show what happens during and after the ordeal. Use Source 4 to help you.

The priest blesses the water

NOTE

If the man sinks below the water then he is innocent. But if he floats he is guilty because evil spirits are holding him up.

Changes in the King's courts

Trial by ordeal was used in England before the Normans arrived. The Normans introduced a new way of asking for God's judgement: trial by battle. In this method the accuser and the accused fight it out. If the accused loses he is punished. If he wins he is freed.

By the thirteenth century changes were taking place in the King's courts. They became more efficient. The king sent experienced judges around the country to visit each area two or three times each year. At these courts the juries had to decide if someone was guilty or not.

Trial by ordeal was abolished in 1215 because the Church was against it. Trial by battle was still used but not very often. If a case could not be proved then juries had to make a decision based on what they knew about the person's character and circumstances.

You can read about the justice two people received from a King's court in Norfolk in the 1300s in Sources 5 and 7.

▲ **SOURCE 6** *From Hampshire Court Records of 1249. Walter Bloweberme and Hamo Stare in 'trial by battle'. Walter accused Hamo of being a thief. Walter won the battle. At the top left you can see what happened to Hamo after the battle*

▼ **SOURCE 7**

Roger of Lynford was taken for stealing three chickens worth 4d. The jurors say that Robert did steal one chicken and one hen worth 2d but the value of the goods is not enough to make them want to convict him. Therefore he is acquitted.

▼ **SOURCE 5**

William was taken for stealing seven pairs of hose. He stands trial and is convicted. He is to be hanged.

▼ **ACTIVITY**

Do you think people in the Middle Ages could get justice? Write two or three sentences to answer this question. Think about:

- **the cases in the manorial court for smaller crimes**
- **trial by ordeal and battle in the early Middle Ages**
- **trials by jury.**

Here are some sentence starters to help you:

In my opinion, the fairest aspects of justice in the Middle Ages were . . .

The least fair aspects were . . .

Changes in the Middle Ages made justice fairer/less fair because . . .

Overall, I think that people in the Middle Ages could/could not get justice because . . .

How to get to Heaven

In the Middle Ages almost everyone believed in Heaven and Hell. On pages 53–61 you will explore how people tried to get to Heaven and avoid going to Hell.

How religious were people in the Middle Ages?

Religion played a very important role in people's lives in the Middle Ages. It was something that was with them every minute of every day.

▼ ACTIVITY

Copy and complete this spider diagram to show the ways in which religion played an important part in medieval people's lives:

RELIGION WAS IMPORTANT BECAUSE ...

God

People believed that God controlled every part of their lives. God made them healthy or ill. If they were successful in their work or business, it was God who had helped them.

The Church was there at the important stages of their lives. At birth babies had to be baptised. Marriage was a special religious service. The last rites were given to the dying.

Everybody had to go to church on Sundays and holy days. All around the village there were SHRINES and holy crosses.

Religion shaped what went on during the year. People looked forward to feasts on special holy days such as Christmas, Easter and CANDLEMAS.

Every villager had to give the Church a TITHE, that is, one tenth of everything they produced. So, if they harvested ten sheaves of corn, they would give one to the priest.

God decided whether you went to Heaven (eternal bliss and happiness) or to Hell (eternal pain and suffering). So pleasing God in your daily life was pretty important!

A vision of Heaven and Hell

Most people in the Middle Ages could not read the Bible for themselves or understand church services because they were in Latin. So one way they learned about the teachings of the Church was from wall paintings (murals) which could be found in most churches.

The painting below shows a ladder rising through Hell and finally reaching Heaven. The souls of dead men and women are trying to climb the ladder to get to Heaven. People were desperate to keep out of Hell where they would remain in agony for the rest of time – eternity.

▼ **SOURCE 1** *A medieval wall painting from a church in Surrey*

▲ SOURCE 2

▼ DISCUSS

1 a) The bottom part of the painting in Source 1 shows what happens to people in Hell. In a group, match each of the descriptions below with one of the letters on the outline drawing of the painting (Source 2):

- murderers being put into a pot of boiling water
- a money lender burning on flames, still counting his gold
- a bridge of spikes for dishonest tradesmen (can you see which tradesmen are shown?)
- demons pulling people off the ladder
- a woman having her hand bitten by a dog. She is confessing to pampering her own dogs with meat when poor people were going hungry
- a drunken pilgrim drinking from a wine bottle.

b) The top half of the painting shows things happening in Heaven. Match each of the descriptions below with one of the letters on the drawing:

- Christ defeating the devil who has his hands tied
- St Michael weighing people's goodness to see if they should go to Heaven or Hell (What do you think the demon on the left is doing?)
- angels helping people up the ladder.

2 Do you think this painting was trying to show that it is easy to get to Heaven or very difficult?

3 How do you think you would have felt if you had been a medieval peasant in church looking at this painting? Would you have been terrified, amused, worried or bored?

HOW TO GET TO HEAVEN

People in the Middle Ages were anxious to get to Heaven and avoid the torments of Hell. To get to Heaven people had to be free of sin. Since most people committed sins during their lives they had to find a way of paying for them – they had to confess their sins and feel genuinely sorry for committing them. There were a number of ways they could do this ...

Route 1 – the priest

I can help you ... come to church ... confess your sins.

▼ ACTIVITY A

As you work through this enquiry, make brief notes about what people had to do to get to Heaven by different routes. At the end of this enquiry, you are going to use these notes to help some medieval people get to Heaven. The first one has been started for you.

ROUTE 1
The priest
- Attend church every Sunday
- Confess your sins

The men who were meant to help people live good lives were the priests. They were meant to be special people. They were not allowed to marry as they had to devote their lives to God. They had special powers like being able to forgive people their sins. They were also meant to help the poor and the sick.

The most important thing to do to get to Heaven was to attend a church service, called Mass, every Sunday. Also people could confess their sins to the priest and he would forgive them. This meant they were free of sin. Priests encouraged people to help others, like the sick and homeless. Good deeds could help you get to Heaven. Bad deeds could send you to Hell. Sources 3 and 4 are stories told by priests to their congregations.

Some travellers, such as MERCHANTS, were often worried that they might die on their journey before they had been to Mass. So priests held Mass at three o'clock in the morning before travellers set out.

Not all priests were good ones. Some behaved disgracefully, for example drinking in taverns, living with women and taking church money for themselves.

Many priests did not live in their parishes. They often had more than one parish, and as they could not live in all of them they appointed deputies to do their work.

There was once a worthy woman who had hated a poor woman for more than seven years. When the worthy woman went to church, the priest told her to forgive her enemy. She said she had forgiven her.

When the church service was over, the woman said (to her neighbours), 'Do you think I forgave her with my heart as I did with my mouth? No!' Then the Devil came down and strangled her there in front of everybody. So make sure that when you make promises you make them with the heart, without any deceit.

▼ SOURCE 4

A woman lived with a priest and bore him three sons. After the priest died, the sons tried to persuade their mother to ask forgiveness for her deadly sin, but she refused.

The mother died soon after and for three nights the sons sat by her body. On the first night, at midnight, to their terror, the bier began to shake. On the second night it shook again and suddenly a devil appeared, seized the corpse, and dragged it towards the door. The sons fought to win the body back and tied it to the bier to keep it safe. On the third night at midnight a whole host of devils invaded the house and took the body, no one knows where, without end forevermore.

▼ ACTIVITY B

1 **Do you think the woman in Source 3 would go to Heaven? Explain your answer.**
2 **Why do you think the woman in Source 4 was seized by devils?**
3 **Why do you think priests told stories like these in church?**

HOW TO GET TO HEAVEN

Route 2 – pilgrimages

> I know you are tired. We have come a long way. The saints will reward us for visiting their shrines.

In the *Canterbury Tales*, Chaucer wrote about a group of pilgrims travelling to Canterbury (see Source 6). They included a merchant from Suffolk, a villein from Norfolk, a nun and a ploughman. One of the group, the Wife of Bath, had been to Rome, to Compostela (in Spain) and to Jerusalem three times.

Guide books were even written for the pilgrims, as journeys were long and could be dangerous.

For those who could not afford overseas trips, there were shrines all over England. The most popular were the shrine of Our Lady at Walsingham, where there was a special statue of Mary and the baby Jesus, and the shrine of St Thomas at Canterbury (see pages 80–86).

When a manor official called at the village of Snailwell to collect the rents in the fifteenth century, he found that 'nearly everybody in the village had gone on pilgrimage to Canterbury'.

Another way of showing you were sorry for your sins was to go on a PILGRIMAGE to the shrine of a great saint. The longer and harder the journey the more repentant (sorry) you showed yourself to be. People believed that sometimes just by going to a holy place or touching a special object there these saints could help you get to Heaven.

▼ **SOURCE 5** *An account by a visitor to England in the late fifteenth century*

The Virgin Mary is very famous all over England. You can find hardly anybody in that island who thinks he can do well unless he makes some present to that Lady every year.

▼ ACTIVITY A

Make your notes on how pilgrimages could help you get to Heaven.

ROUTE 2
Pilgrimages

Route 3 – buying your way to Heaven

Buy this and God will forgive your sins.

People believed that nearly everyone went to Purgatory when they died. This was not quite as awful as Hell. To move from Purgatory to Heaven you had to be sorry for your sins, and get people who were still alive to pray for you.

People often left money for prayers to be said for them after they were dead (see Source 8). Rich people paid for colleges to be set up, where priests did nothing but pray for their soul and perhaps for other dead members of their family.

The less well-off paid to join guilds (associations) which would arrange to hold masses (church services) for their soul after they died. There were over 100 of these guilds in Northamptonshire alone.

▼ **SOURCE 7** *The description of the Pardoner from Chaucer's* Canterbury Tales

He'd sewed a holy relic on his cap;
his wallet lay before him on his lap,
brimful of pardons come from Rome.
In his trunk he had a pillow case
which he claimed was Our Lady's veil.

▼ **SOURCE 8** *Extracts from medieval wills*

To the Rood Loft 6s 7d
to the bells 12d
to the torches 12d
I will that 30 masses be said for my soul and all Christian souls after my death.

▼ **SOURCE 6** *This picture shows pilgrims from Chaucer's poem* Canterbury Tales *about a group of people on a pilgrimage to Canterbury*

If you had enough money you could try to buy your way to Heaven. Pardoners travelled the country selling pardons. These freed people from their sins. This meant they would go straight to Heaven when they died.

▼ **ACTIVITY B**

1 **Make your notes on all the ways you could buy your way to Heaven.**

2 **Which of routes 1–3 would be open to:**
   a) poor people
   b) fairly well-off people
   c) rich people?

▼ **DISCUSS**

3 **Do you think rich people had a better chance or a worse chance of getting to Heaven?**

ROUTE 3
Buying your way to Heaven

Route 4 – becoming a nun or a monk

Join us and cleanse your soul.

Some people in the Middle Ages decided to devote their whole life to God and became monks or nuns. They took solemn vows:

- not to marry
- to have no possessions and live simple lives
- to do whatever the abbot (chief monk) or abbess (chief nun) told them.

Their daily lives were lived by strict rules (see Sources 9 and 10). In England there were about 130 nunneries, and thousands of monasteries.

▼ **SOURCE 9** *The daily timetable followed by nuns*

2 a.m. Religious services until dawn, when returned to bed and slept for three hours
6 a.m. Got up; services followed until 12 noon
12 noon until 5 p.m. Working on the farm, e.g. haymaking and digging
5 p.m. until 7 p.m. More services; then straight to bed.

Nunneries

Most of the nunneries were small. Only four had over 30 nuns, and many had less than ten. Although the nunneries were not rich, most nuns came from rich families. For many of these women it was the only alternative to marriage, and some women became nuns after they were widowed. It was very rare for peasant women to go into a nunnery. They were needed too badly in the fields.

The nuns had three meals a day. In the morning they had bread and ale, and for dinner at midday they had beef, pork or bacon. The Bible was read to them while they ate their dinner. Supper in the evening was usually a light meal of fish. The nuns had to remain silent nearly all the time and communicated by sign language.

Monasteries

Some monasteries were very large. As well as being places to live and work, they were places where the sick and the poor could be cared for by the monks.

▼ **SOURCE 10** *Abbot Ailred on life in Rievaulx Abbey in 1135*

Our food is scanty, our garments rough; our drink is from the stream. Under our tired limbs there is but a hard mat; when sleep is sweetest we must rise at a bell's bidding. There is no moment for idleness.

▼ **ACTIVITY A**

ROUTE 4
Being a nun or a monk

1 **Why were many nuns from rich families?**
2 **Write down three ways that being a monk or nun meant that your life was hard and strict.**
3 **How do you think this hard life would help a monk or a nun get to Heaven? Write your answer in your notes.**

▼ ACTIVITY B

1 Work in pairs or groups. On the right you can see some medieval people. They all want to get to Heaven. Your task is to recommend TWO ways each person can do this. Decide which ways you think are the most suitable for the different characters. Be prepared to present your ideas to the rest of the class. The notes you have collected will help you do this.

2 You now have a choice of activities. Remember you are still working in pairs or groups.

Either
Design and decorate a guide book for people in the Middle Ages to show them the routes by which they can get to Heaven. Since many of them cannot read, you will have to rely on drawings. This should include things that they *should not do* as well as things they *should do.*

Or
Design a decorated route to Heaven for a medieval wall display (like a wall painting). One idea is that this could be a road on which you can do things to help you progress to Heaven.

▼ DISCUSS

3 Why did the Church have such a powerful influence over people in the Middle Ages?

Is religion more or less important to people today as it was then?

A villein and his wife, poor hardworking peasants

A rich merchant who travels around a great deal

The wife of a nobleman who died in the Crusades. She tried to run the estate but became poor when the harvest failed

A tradesman and his wife. They are not well off but have worked hard and have a little spare money

How to get to Heaven

What problems did travellers face in the Middle Ages?

▶▶ **Travelling in the Middle Ages was not always easy. On pages 62–65 you will write a report for the King on the problems faced by travellers.**

▼ **ACTIVITY**

Nicholas and Sarah have to transport their wool from Derby to the market in London, where merchants will buy it to send abroad. They load their wool up onto packhorses and set off. They meet many other travellers with horses and wagons on the road.

Imagine that during their journey Nicholas and Sarah meet all the problems referred to in Sources 2–6.

Your task is to write five diary entries describing the problems they meet, and how they overcome them.

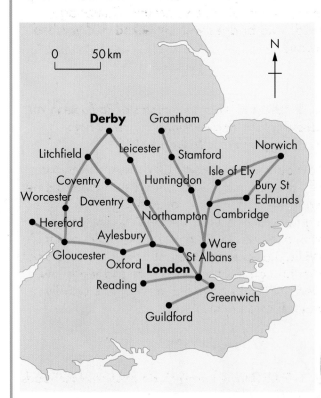

▲ **SOURCE 1** *A map showing the main routes through medieval England around 1360. Some of the routes are on the same lines as the old Roman roads. Nicholas and Sarah's route is marked in red*

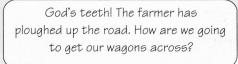

God's teeth! The farmer has ploughed up the road. How are we going to get our wagons across?

▼ SOURCE 2

The roads were very bad indeed, because no one mended them. Farmers ploughed some of them, and in bad weather most of the roads became impossible to use.

▼ SOURCE 3 *From fifteenth-century town records*

At Aylesbury, the local miller dug clay out of the road, creating a pit so large that a glove seller passing through the town fell into it and was drowned.

▼ SOURCE 4 *A description of the roads in 1406*

This year has been remarkable for terrible floods and rains. The roads between London and Greenwich were broken. The cartway between Whitney Bridge and Hereford was nearly swept away. In the Isle of Ely, around Cambridge, roads and bridges were wrecked and washed away.

▼ SOURCE 5 *From the records of Parliament. An account of an incident during a journey from Northamptonshire to London in 1450*

160 persons and more, all dressed in the form of war with light helmets, long swords and other weapons, hid under a large hedge next to the highway and lay in wait for William Tresham from midnight to the hour of six, at which time William appeared. They attacked him and smote him through the body and foot and more. He died. And they gave him many more deadly wounds and cut his throat.

▼ SOURCE 6 *A traveller's description of the roads in 1400*

Travellers often lose their way and go ways which are unknown. Therefore knots are often made in the branches of trees and bushes to mark the highway.

Improving the roads

Some attempts were made to make the roads better to travel on. Work out what improvements were suggested in Sources 7–9 below.

> This is a lot better than it used to be. Now we can be sure there is nobody waiting in the bushes to rob us.

▼ **SOURCE 7** *In 1285 the King and Parliament passed the Statute of Winchester*

Highways leading from one market town to another shall be widened where there are bushes or ditches, so that there will be no bushes or ditches for a man to hide to do hurt within 200 feet [60 metres] of the road.

▼ **SOURCE 8** *From the Records of the Borough of Nottingham, 1370*

The King allows the mayors of Nottingham to start a ferry service across the River Trent, on condition that all the profits shall be used on the repairing of the bridge, which has been broken for over 70 years.

▼ **SOURCE 9** *A letter from King Edward I to the Prior and people of Dunstable in 1285*

Because we have learnt that the high roads which stretch through Dunstable are so broken up by the frequent passage of carts, that dangerous injuries threaten those using these roads, we command each one of you according to his means to fill in and mend the roads.

▼ **ACTIVITY A**

Use the writing frame below, or your own ideas, to write a report for the King on the problems travellers face and how the solutions in Sources 7 – 9 might help.

> Sire,
>
> I beg leave to submit my report on the state of the roads and by-ways of England. I am afraid, my liege, that the roads are in a parlous state. In many places the roads have . . .
>
> Other problems travellers face that can make their journey difficult and dangerous are . . .
>
> Finally, I have some suggestions for ways we might encourage people to improve the roads. Firstly . . .

Methods of transport

▲ **SOURCE 10** *Packhorses carrying woolpacks. A painting from the thirteenth century*

▲ **SOURCE 11** *A picture of a harvest wagon drawn in the early fourteenth century. Notice the spiked wheels*

▲ **SOURCE 12** *Unloading grain from a barge. This picture was drawn in the late fifteenth century*

▼ **ACTIVITY B**

1 Look at Sources 10 and 11. How are these two methods of transport different?
2 Which method do you think is the best
   a) on good roads in and around towns
   b) over rough country or where the roads are bad?
3 Look at Sources 12 and 13. What would be
   a) the advantages,
   b) the disadvantages
   of transporting goods by water?

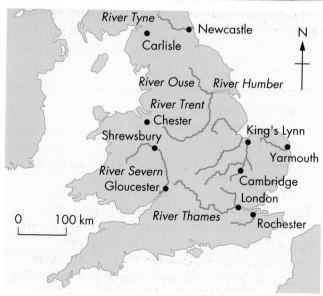

▲ **SOURCE 13** *Main river routes in England*

▲ **65**

Can you survive in the town?

▶▶ In the Middle Ages most people lived in villages. But there were some small towns. People from nearby villages came to town to buy and sell goods in the market. First you are going to look at a real town, Ludlow, then you will play a board game based on life in a medieval town and finally use your own research to add extra elements to the game.

Step 1: Get to know a town

The year is 1250. Welcome to Ludlow! It is very different from Wharram Percy on page 34.

▼ ACTIVITY

Work in pairs.

1 Draw a quick sketch of your partner no bigger than a one pence piece.
2 Now cut it out and place it somewhere interesting on the picture in Source 1.
3 Still in pairs, describe to each other what is around you in the town. What can you see? What can you hear? What can you smell?
4 Compare this town with the village of Wharram Percy on page 34. Draw up a list of similarities and differences.
5 Where would you prefer to live: Ludlow or Wharram Percy? Explain your reasons.

Two hundred years ago there was nothing here except this bridge over the river Teme.

Some parts of the town are well kept and clean. Other parts are cramped, dirty and smelly. On market day there are as many animals as people. There are no sewers so rubbish and excrement sometimes litter the streets.

The lord taxes everyone who trades in the market. The lord gets richer but so do the traders.

▶ SOURCE 1

In 1100 this strong castle was built by a powerful lord to control the river crossing.

In the early 1200s the lord started this neatly planned town around the castle. He got permission from the King to hold a market every week.

It is a good market. People come from miles around to trade here. Local villages send their surplus goods such as eggs, cheese or vegetables. At the market the villagers buy things they can not make at home – such as shoes, cloth or cooking pots.

Ludlow's speciality is everything to do with sheep, wool and woollen cloth. There are twelve mills in the town.

Step 2: Play 'The Town Game'

One big attraction of towns was freedom. In the village a villein's whole life was controlled by the lord of the manor.
A town offered a chance to escape. All towns had different rules but in some towns if a villein lived in the town for a year and a day he could become a freeman.

▼ **ACTIVITY**

Some villeins have come to town. If they can survive here for a year and a day then they become freemen. To survive they have to:

- earn some money
- find somewhere to live
- stay healthy.

Does this sound easy? Well play 'The Town Game' and find out just what could go wrong for a villein in search of his freedom.

How to play 'The Town Game'

1. Play the game in groups of two, three or four. Two is the quickest. Four is best.
2. You will need: a dice, a playing piece for each player and some tokens (which count as money).
3. Throw the dice and move your playing piece around the board following the instructions on each square. (For Chance squares see below).
4. Your aim is to survive for a whole year – or four times round the board.
5. At the start you receive two tokens. You earn and spend more tokens as you move around the board. At the end you need at least one token to buy your freedom, so don't run out of tokens if you can avoid it.
6. Very important: you can't work until you find somewhere to live. So until you land on the pigsty, the lodgings or the inn, the work squares do not apply to you. You can do nothing on the work squares.
7. Keep a diary of what happens to you. Your teacher can give you a recording sheet.
8. Keep a tally of each time you pass the Start. You have to go round four times.
9. Everyone who gets to the end with at least one token is given their freedom.
10. The winner is the person who survives to the end and has the most tokens.

Chance squares

What happens on a Chance square? To start with nothing happens – this is a rest square. But after you have played the game once and learned the (simple) rules you will then create your own Chance cards based on evidence from the Middle Ages. You can find out how to do this on pages 70–71.

START

Feast day

Rich people are giving out charity to the poor. Collect 2 tokens as you pass.

Freedom?

The lord of your village has sent men to look for you. You are his best worker and he wants you back. You go into hiding. Miss a turn.

Work

If you have already got at least five tokens you can hire a cart and set up a carting business. Earn another five tokens and throw again.

Danger

You have broken your leg. You cannot work or even look for work. Miss two turns.

CHANCE

Will you be lucky?

The inn

Expensive but more comfortable than the pigsty or the lodgings. Pay 2 tokens or move back to the pigsty. Now you can look for work. Throw again.

Work

The town walls are being mended. There is plenty of work quarrying and carrying stones. Earn 5 tokens and throw again.

THE TOWN GAME

Freedom?

You go to confession to tell the priest that you have been missing Mass. He orders you to spend time praying. Miss a turn.

CHANCE

Will you be lucky?

Freedom ?

You fall in love. Since you will soon be free of the lord you decide to marry. You spend half your tokens on a celebration.

Danger

Excrement falls on your head from a toilet above a pathway – you fall ill with dysentery. Miss a turn.

Danger

Your lodgings catch fire. You survive but you lose all your tokens and you have to find somewhere else to live before you can work again.

CHANCE

Will you be lucky?

Work

Clean up after market. Earn 2 tokens and throw again.

The pigsty

You can sleep here in return for looking after some pigs. Horrible but warm and free. Now you can look for work. Throw again.

CHANCE

Will you be lucky?

Work

You have brought your best cow to town with you. Sell milk in exchange for 2 tokens. Throw again.

Danger

You get beaten up by some town thugs who don't like newcomers. Lose all your tokens (except one which you had hidden in your boot). Miss a turn.

Taxation

If you have tokens pay half to the town. If you have no tokens hide – you might be thrown out for being a vagrant. Miss a turn.

Lodgings

You find a room for rent. Pay 1 token or, if you can't afford that, move back to the pigsty. Now you can look for work. Throw again.

CAN YOU SURVIVE IN THE TOWN?

Step 3: Make 'The Town Game' better

Now that you know how 'The Town Game' works you probably have ideas on how to improve it. You can start by making some Chance cards. You should base these cards on things that really happened in the Middle Ages. Below and on the facing page you can see some evidence and information that you could use for your research. You could use other books or the computer as well. Try not to repeat things that are already on 'The Town Game' board.

One foot in the grave!

Many people in towns suffered from poor diet and poor health. Plague regularly hit towns. Diseases spread rapidly in the cramped and dirty conditions. Childbirth was a particularly dangerous time for women and for infants.

What's that coming out of your eye?

Many people were infected by worms. These were parasites a few centimetres long which lived in your body. Sometimes these could come out of your body – there are accounts of them crawling out of people's eyes. Worms were embarrassing, but they also sapped your energy and stopped you working. They were passed from person to person through infected food or water.

▼ ACTIVITY

How to make a Chance card
You could follow your own design but this is how we suggest you design a Chance card.

- **Describe the problem using the examples shown opposite or from your own research.**
- **Describe two possible outcomes: a good one and a bad one.**

When they pick up a Chance card players will roll the dice. If they throw 1–3 the bad thing happens. If they throw 4–6 the good thing happens. For example:

> ### Chance
> You catch a fever. There is no one in the town you can turn to. You decide to walk home to your village for help. Will you survive?
>
> ### Throw a dice
> **1–3** Bad luck: you are too weak. You die by the roadside on the way home. Your game is over.
> **4–6** Good news: you get back to your village. You are given some herbal remedies. The fever passes. You are quickly able to return to town.

Pay up!

To make money for the town the local lord and the town officials used to charge a tax on each sale in the market. For example, every time someone sold a roll of cloth or a cow they had to pay the town one penny.

Join the Guild!

Traders such as shoemakers, leather workers, goldsmiths, and even fishmongers set up GUILDS to protect their businesses. To work in this trade you *had* to belong to the guild, follow the guild rules and meet their standards. Anyone not in the guild was forbidden from working in that trade and could be hounded out of town if they tried.

▼ SOURCE 2 *Some of the rules of a guild*

If a member of the guild lived in adultery, none of the other members of the guild were to have anything to do with him.

No outsiders were allowed to sell cloth within the town.

No member could take more than one apprentice at a time.

Get those pigs out of here!

Towns were dirty places. Many people kept animals in the towns just as they had when they lived in the country. In one town someone was elected to herd all the pigs into a pigpen to keep them off the streets.

Get rid of that house!

People built their own houses but the town officials sometimes ordered buildings to be pulled down because they were built in the wrong place, or they were a nuisance, or they wanted the space for something else like a church extension.

What a pong!

Most towns had no sewers. Some streets had a drain running down the middle to carry away the waste which was thrown into the street. Some houses had cellars where all the sewage was dropped until the collectors came to collect it. Sometimes it stayed there for years.

Improvements needed!

Successful towns found that as more people came to the town they needed to improve it. For example so many people were using the bridge at Ludlow that a second one was needed. Meanwhile anyone with a boat could make a good living out of ferrying people and animals across the river. The town made lots of money charging a toll each time someone used the bridge.

Shame on you!

A town didn't want people selling shoddy goods at inflated prices or cheating their customers and giving the market a bad name. Dishonest traders could be paraded through the streets and put in the pillory or the stocks. For example:

▼ **SOURCE 3** *From London Court Records, 1327*

John Bird the baker did skilfully cause a hole to be made upon a table in his bakehouse. And when his neighbours and others, who were wont to bake their bread at his oven, came with their dough, John put the dough on the table. John had a servant sitting in secret beneath the table. The servant carefully opened the hole and bit by bit withdrew some of the dough.

All those bakers beneath whose tables holes had been found should be put on the pillory, with dough hung from their necks, and those bakers whose tables did not have holes shall be put on the pillory, but without dough round their necks.

Even harder for a woman!

Women had fewer options than men. Their main trade was brewing ale. Women also worked in metal working and cloth making. But women were not allowed to join guilds. The leather workers for example even forbade widows from carrying on their husband's work after he died.

Was the Black Death a disaster?

On pages 72–77 you will look at how the Black Death arrived in England and the terrible effect it had. You are going to finish off this story ...

It is 1348, the year of the Black Death.
The scene is a cottage in a village near Southampton ...

Alice recoiled from the smell as she entered the cottage. Stephen, the man she was going to marry, lay writhing in agony on the bed. He had cast off the blanket covering him revealing, to her horror, huge black boils in his armpits and black spots on his arms.

The source of the smell was not hard to detect. One of the boils had burst and an evil-smelling black pus was oozing out. Even as she stood there staring, unable to move, a second boil exploded sending out a stream of black filth. Despite her disgust and the nausea that rose in her throat, Alice moved towards the bed. Stephen saw her and cried out 'Stay away! Stay away! Call the priest! I must make my last confession. God is punishing me for my sins! Oh, this terrible thirst!'

As Alice ran to the church, she went over the events of the last few days in her mind. Was it only five days ago that Stephen, her Stephen, had arrived in the village for their marriage! He drove wagons for a wool merchant in Southampton. The merchant had recently received a shipment of fine cloth from Italy and Stephen's job was to cart it to the towns served by the great port of Southampton. He had pulled out some of the cloth to show her, joking that it would make a fine wedding dress. A dead rat had fallen out and Stephen said that there seemed to be lots of rats in the city at the moment.

He had told her tales of a terrible sickness that was striking people down in Southampton, how people were running away from the city into the surrounding countryside taking their belongings with them. Most people, he had said, believed it was a punishment from God, but some blamed the Jews and foreigners in the city.

Little did they think it would affect them – they lived simple lives, went to Mass each Sunday and did nobody any harm. But shortly after Stephen had arrived home he developed a fever. The next day he complained of terrible pains in his groin and armpits. And now ... dear God ... what was this horrible illness!

What was the Black Death?

People in medieval England always faced famine and disease, but in the middle of the fourteenth century they had to survive the Black Death. It spread from Asia to Europe and then to England, where over one-third of the population died. At that time doctors did not know about germs causing diseases, but they did have their own ideas about the Black Death.

Some historians think that there were two different PLAGUES at this time:

Bubonic plague

The germ is carried in the bloodstream of rats. The fleas which bite the rats become infected and when they leave the rats for more food they often bite humans and pass on the plague. These fleas multiply in warm weather but die off in cold weather, so bubonic plague does not spread very widely in the winter. Sufferers develop a fever and buboes (swellings) in the groin and in the armpit. About 70 per cent of patients die. It takes between four and seven days for them to die.

Pneumonic plague

This plague is caught through breathing. It attacks the lungs. Patients cough blood and spray out germs every time they breathe out. It kills everyone infected within two days and is not affected by the weather or climate.

▼ **SOURCE 1** *Medieval descriptions of the plague*

a) Apostumes and carbuncles on the armpits and the groin. From this, one died in five days.

b) Continuous fever and spitting of blood. Men suffer in their lungs and breathing, and whoever has been corrupted cannot live beyond two days or three days.

c) The emergence of certain tumours in the groin or armpits, some of which grew as large as a common apple. Black spots appeared on the arm or the thigh.

d) Anyone who is infected by it dies, all who see him in his sickness, quickly follow thither.

▼ ACTIVITY

1 Look at Source 1. What type of plague does each extract describe? Give reasons for your answer.
2 Explain how the plague was passed on to humans from rats.
3 From what you know about living conditions in villages and towns, do you think diseases like the plague would have spread easily?

WAS THE BLACK DEATH A DISASTER?

▲ **SOURCE 2** *A medieval painting showing the Black Death as a rider on horseback*

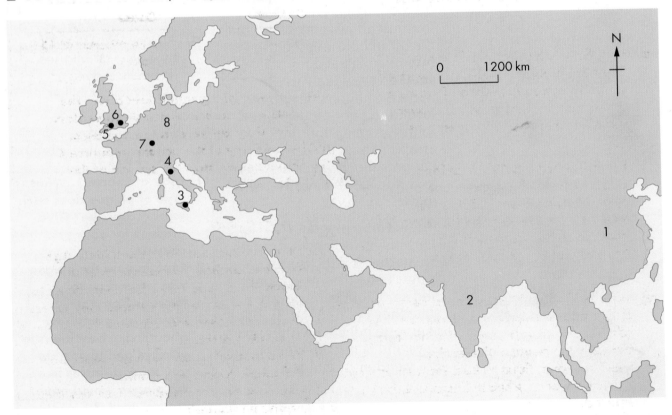

▲ **SOURCE 3** *A map showing the spread of the plague*

▼ **SOURCE 4** *Medieval descriptions of the spread of the plague*

a) In 1347 twelve galleys entered the harbour of Messina (Sicily). In their bones the sailors bore so virulent a disease that anyone who only spoke to them was seized by a deadly illness.

b) In 1348 that memorable mortality happened here in Florence. It was sent upon us by the just anger of God. The city was cleansed of much filth, and sickly persons were banned from entering, but nothing prevented it.

c) Jews were burned in Strasbourg in 1349. It was believed that the Jews had caused the plague by poisoning drinking water.

d) In 1345, in China and India, fire fell from heaven and stinking smoke, which slew all that were left of men and beasts. By these winds the whole province was infected.

e) Flagellants whipped themselves in Germany early in 1349. They believed that the plague was sent by God as a punishment for human sin. They were punishing themselves for these sins.

f) 1349. To the Lord Mayor of London. Order to cause the human dung and other filth lying in the streets to be removed. The city is so foul with the filth from out of the houses that the air is infected and the city poisoned.

g) In June 1348, in Melcombe, in the county of Dorset, two ships came alongside. One of the sailors had brought with him from Gascony the seeds of the terrible pestilence and, through him, the men of that town were the first in England to be infected.

▼ **ACTIVITY**

1 **Look at Source 2 carefully.**
   a) **What does the skeleton represent?**
   b) **Why do you think the skeleton is riding a horse?**
   c) **Which of these two statements do you think is correct?**

   ■ **The artist is saying that poor people were more likely to catch the Black Death.**
   ■ **The artist is saying that the Black Death hits the rich and poor alike.**

2 **Match each of the extracts in Source 4 with the correct place number on the map (Source 3). An atlas will help you. Look carefully at the dates of each extract. Then write a short account called 'The Spread of the Plague'.**

3 **Read the extracts in Source 4. Now copy and complete the table below to show what medieval people thought had caused the Black Death. An example has been done for you.**

Extract	Cause
c)	Jews poisoned drinking water

4 **Use everything you know about the beliefs of medieval people to explain why they believed in these causes.**

5 **Would any of the actions in Source 4 have helped stop the spread of the plague?**

▼ **DISCUSS**

6 **'The fact that people in the Middle Ages believed in these explanations of the Black Death, and used these measures to stop it, just shows how stupid they were!' Discuss whether you agree or disagree with this statement.**

7 **Were medieval people simply stupid or do people today give similar explanations for diseases? Can you think of any examples?**

WAS THE BLACK DEATH A DISASTER?

Historians think that the Black Death killed over one-third of the people of England. There were not enough villeins left to farm the land so crops were left to rot in the fields. Villages were deserted. Some villages, like Wharram Percy, never recovered. They simply rotted away and disappeared.

But it was not all bad news for the peasants who survived the Black Death as you can see below.

Higher wages
Lords could not get enough labourers to work on their land. They were so desperate that they were prepared to pay higher wages.

More land and low rents
Peasants were able to bargain with lords to farm more land at lower rents because there was so much unworked land around.

No labour services
In some places peasants stopped doing their labour services – boon-work and week-work (see page 40). Often they gave the lord a low payment instead. Lords did not complain because they wanted to keep the peasants on their manors.

Better offers
Lords tried to poach peasants from other manors by offering them higher wages.

TO THE MANOR OF

More freedom
Peasants had more freedom of movement because they could go and work for someone else.

▼ ACTIVITY

1 **Look at the three cartoons here. Decide which people are peasants and which are lords or officials. On a separate piece of paper write captions for the three cartoons and complete the speech bubbles.**

I can afford new tools now because...

They've all gone to work for someone else because...

That's right. I'm offering you double wages because...

2 **Working in groups, write the script for, and act out, a short play which continues the story that started on page 72.**

Here are some ideas about how you could begin to plan your play:

Scene 1

- Stephen dies/does not die . . .
- The villagers are frightened . . .

Scene 2

The villagers try to stop the plague spreading . . .
- What do they do to Stephen's cottage?
- Do they try to block the village so that no other travellers can come in?

Scene 3

The plague begins to spread through the village . . .
- Does Alice catch the plague?
- What happens as more people become ill?

Scene 4

The plague is over. Many households have lost members of the family . . .
- Who survives in Alice's family?
- Who leaves the village? Who stays?
- Does anything good come out of the plague?

Although you are making your play up, you must try and keep to the evidence and information about the Black Death in this section. Try to remember that medieval people would not have known much about the sickness.

Review: Living in medieval times

Imagine that you are a researcher helping to design 'The Medieval Experience' theme park. The idea of the theme park is that visitors come for a day to get a flavour of village life in the Middle Ages.

You know a lot about life in the Middle Ages. As medieval experts you have to draw up some plans for the park.

Unlike some theme parks the organisers are interested in trying to be accurate.

Plan an exhibit
The organisers want customers to visit a number of medieval buildings. Your task is as follows.

1 a) Describe one of these buildings: it could be a peasant's cottage, a manor house, a mill, a church or some other building you have found out about on pages 32–77. It must be as accurate as possible.
   b) You should explain to the organisers how the building should sound and smell so that it is like it would be in the Middle Ages.
   c) Who would be in the building? What would they be doing – cooking, conducting a trial, praying?
   d) You could also describe the costumes which the workers in the theme park should wear to look like they belong in the Middle Ages.
   e) Attach drawings or sources to your plan to help the organisers visualise it.

2 Once you have completed your own plans, look at other people's exhibits and suggest improvements to their plans. If you think they have got anything wrong explain:
   a) what they have got wrong
   b) how you know they are wrong
   c) what evidence you have that they are wrong.

SECTION 4

PROBLEMS FACING MEDIEVAL KINGS

A king's nightmare!

It was not always easy being a king in the Middle Ages. Kings had to deal with major problems. If they made the wrong decisions they could throw the country into chaos or threaten their own lives. In this section you are going to investigate three big problems: the Church, the barons and the peasants, and see how kings dealt with each one.

Then you will come back to this picture and create 'the King's nightmare'. How scary can it be?

Powerful barons ...

Angry peasants ...

Bossy bishops ...

It's not easy being a king.

Murder in the cathedral

▶▶ In 1170 the Archbishop of Canterbury, Thomas Becket, was murdered in Canterbury Cathedral. On pages 80–86 you will be looking at the reasons why this murder took place.

The murder

◀ SOURCE 1 *A thirteenth-century painting of Becket's death*

▼ SOURCE 2 *This account is by William Fitzstephen. He was Becket's clerk and friend*

One of the knights struck him with the flat of his sword between the shoulders, saying, 'Fly, you are a dead man.' The knights tried to drag him out of the church. But the monks held him back.

Edward Grim, one of the monks, putting his arm up, received the first stroke of the sword and was severely wounded. By this same stroke the ARCHBISHOP was wounded in the head.

As he knelt down clasping and stretching his hands out to God, a second stroke was dealt him on the head, at which he fell by the altar.

While he lay there Richard Brito struck him with such force that the sword was broken against his head. Four wounds in all did the saintly Archbishop receive.

The whole of the crown of his head was lopped off. But he didn't try to avoid or parry the blows. He accepted death from a desire to be with God.

Hugh of Horsea extracted the blood and brains from the hollow of his head with the point of a sword.

▼ SOURCE 3 *This account is by Edward Grim, a priest, who was with Becket at the time of his death*

The murderers came in full armour, with swords and axes. The monks cried out to the Archbishop to flee to the church. But he had long since yearned for martyrdom and dreaded that it would be delayed if he fled to the church. But the monks pulled, dragged and pushed him into the church. The four knights followed with rapid strides. The Archbishop ordered the doors of the church to be kept open.

In a spirit of mad fury the knights called out, 'Where is Thomas Becket, traitor to the King and the country?' At this he quite unafraid came down the steps and answered, 'Here I am, no traitor to the King, but a priest.'

Having said this he stood by a pillar.

'You shall die this instant,' they cried.

They pulled and dragged him violently, trying to get him outside the church. But they could not get him away from the pillar. Then he inclined his head as one in prayer and joined his hands together and uplifted them.

The wicked knight leapt suddenly upon him and wounded him in the head.

Next he received a second blow on the head, but still he stood firm.

At the third blow he fell on his knees and elbows, saying in a low voice, 'For the name of Jesus I am ready to die.'

The next blow separated the crown of his head and the blood white with the brain and the brain red with the blood stained the floor.

The fourth knight warded off any who sought to interfere.

A fifth man placed his foot on the neck of the holy priest and scattered the brains and blood about the pavement.

▼ ACTIVITY

1 **Compare Sources 1–3 using a copy of the grid below. You will not be able to fill in all the boxes.**

	Source 1	Source 2	Source 3
How many knights were there?			
Where did the murder take place?			
Why couldn't the knights get Beckett out of the church?			
What happened when the first blow was struck?			
What was Becket doing when he was struck?			
Is there evidence that he was afraid of dying?			
Is there evidence that he wanted to die?			

2 **Which give you the best idea of what happened, the written accounts or the painting?**
3 **What evidence is there that both writers were on Becket's side?**
4 **Does this make them less reliable?**

MURDER IN THE CATHEDRAL

▶▶ **In the rest of this enquiry you are going to look at why Thomas Becket was murdered and you are going to write a radio script for your local radio about it.**

Seven steps to the murder

Becket was the son of a Norman merchant. He became Henry II's Chancellor and they grew to be good friends. Thomas became rich and powerful, the second most important man in England. He was loyal to Henry.

Step 1:
Henry had been having some disagreements with the Church. He was not happy with the power the Pope, who lived in Rome, had over the English Church. He was angry that the Pope had said that kings should not appoint bishops. Bishops were very powerful – they had control over a lot of land and people – and Henry wanted to appoint his friends and supporters as bishops. He was even more angry that the Church had its own courts to judge cases involving the clergy. They often gave the clergy light punishments.

Step 2:
In 1162 the Archbishop of Canterbury, the head of the Church in England, died. **Henry decided to make his friend, Thomas, Archbishop**. Then the Church would not cause him so much trouble.

Step 3:
However, it did not work out quite as he expected. **Thomas Becket changed when he was made Archbishop**. He started to live a very religious life. He spent a lot of his time praying and gave up his rich lifestyle.

Step 4:
This shocked Henry. But what was even more shocking to him was that **Becket refused to help him control the Church.** For example he refused to get rid of the Church courts. When Henry passed a law saying that anyone found guilty in a Church court would also be punished in the King's courts, Becket refused to accept it. Henry was furious. Becket, fearing for his safety, ran away to France.

Step 5:
Henry decided to show Becket that he could manage without him. He asked the Archbishop of York to crown his son as the next King of England. This made Becket angry because the crowning of a king had always been the Archbishop of Canterbury's job – his job.

Step 6:
Eventually, in 1170, Henry and Becket met to sort out their problems. Becket agreed to serve the King if he was allowed to come back to England to carry on as Archbishop. However, **as soon as Becket was back he punished all the bishops who had supported the King against him.** He seemed determined to carry on the argument.

Step 7:
When Henry heard about this he flew into a terrible rage. He shouted **'Will no one rid me of this troublesome priest?'** Four knights, loyal to Henry, heard this and decided that it was time to get rid of Becket once and for all. They set off for Canterbury. Later, Henry found out about this and sent some other knights to stop them, but it was too late! You already know what happened next.

▼ ACTIVITY A
The cartoons on the opposite page are jumbled up. Use the story of Thomas Becket to put them in the right order.

▲ Henry became so angry that Thomas fled to France

▲ Thomas had been Henry's loyal friend

▲ Back in England, Thomas Becket did more things that infuriated Henry

▲ Thomas became very religious and took the Church's side against Henry

▲ Henry and Thomas made up their quarrel and Becket returned to England

▲ Henry flew into a rage and said he wanted to be rid of the troublesome priest

▲ Henry made Thomas Archbishop of Canterbury. He thought Thomas would help him control the Church

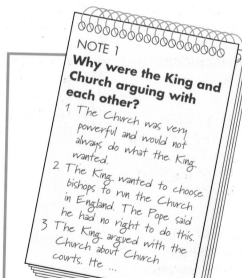

NOTE 1

Why were the King and Church arguing with each other?

1 The Church was very powerful and would not always do what the King wanted.
2 The King wanted to choose bishops to run the Church in England. The Pope said he had no right to do this.
3 The King argued with the Church about Church courts. He ...

NOTE 2

Why did Henry and Becket quarrel?

1 Thomas had been Henry's friend. Henry made him Archbishop of Canterbury to help him control the Church in England.
But ...

▼ ACTIVITY B

1 **Throughout your work on this enquiry you are going to collect information to help you write a radio script. Note 1 has been started for you. Copy the note and finish off the third point.**
2 **Now do the same for Note 2. The first point has been started for you.**

MURDER IN THE CATHEDRAL

How far was the murder to do with personalities?

The previous pages will have given you the impression that the murder was all about controlling the Church. But there was more to it than that. It is a human story.

Henry and Becket had once been friends and Henry felt that Becket had betrayed their friendship. This was a strong relationship gone sour. This may have made him angrier towards Becket.

It was also to do with the type of men they were and their personalities. Both were strong. Henry was determined to control the Church. Becket was equally determined that the King should not. Read Sources 4 and 5.

> ▼ **SOURCE 4** *Written in the 1180s by Gerald of Wales, a bishop*
>
> Henry was a man of reddish, freckled complexion, with a large round head and grey eyes which glowed fiercely and grew bloodshot in anger.

> ▼ **SOURCE 5** *A recent description of Becket*
>
> Becket was a vain, obstinate and ambitious man, who sought always to keep himself in the public eye; he was above all a man of extremes, a man who knew no half measures.

▼ ACTIVITY A

1 **What kind of men do Henry and Becket seem to have been? Do any of these words describe them well: weak, shy, stubborn, unreasonable, bad-tempered, fair, strong-minded, proud, ambitious? Think of any other words you would use to describe them.**

2 **Make notes on the part personal factors and relationships played in the murder.**

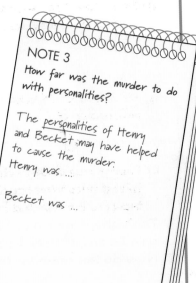

NOTE 3

How far was the murder to do with personalities?

The personalities of Henry and Becket may have helped to cause the murder.

Henry was ...

Becket was ...

Who was to blame for the murder?

▼ ACTIVITY B

1 **Using all you know about the story, think about who was to blame for Becket's death. Draw a chart like the one below. Read the statements on the slips and then put them into the column you think they fit best.**

Who was to blame for the murder of Thomas Becket?		
Henry	The knights	Becket himself

a) He carried on the quarrel after he returned to England and he knew this would put him in danger.

b) They did not have orders from the King. They decided to kill Becket just to gain the King's approval.

c) Henry did not really mean to have Becket killed.

d) They believed Henry really wanted Becket dead and they wanted to please him.

e) He more or less ordered the murder. It was clear to people that he wanted it done.

f) He seemed to want to be a martyr so that he could serve God and the Church.

g) He had a good chance to escape but refused to go.

h) Henry was angry with his former friend who was causing so much trouble. He wanted him dead.

2 **Write down your thoughts about who was to blame on a copy of the note below.**

NOTE 4
Who was to blame for the murder of Thomas Becket?
Henry was to blame because ...

The knights were to blame because ...

Becket was partly to blame for his murder because ...

MURDER IN THE CATHEDRAL

▼ ACTIVITY

1 Work in pairs. It is the anniversary of Thomas Becket's death. The local radio station has asked you to write a programme about the murder for them. Use the notes you have collected to help you prepare the radio script. The programme is in five parts. Some ideas for how you might start are set out below. When you have finished, you might get a chance to present it to the rest of the class.

Part 1
In this part you talk about the argument between Henry and the Church.

Henry II, like many medieval kings, had problems with the Church. He . . .

Part 2
You talk about how Henry came to make Becket Archbishop of Canterbury.

He chose his friend Thomas Becket . . .

Part 3
Explain how the quarrel started between them.

It was not long before they fell out. Becket . . .

Part 4
Explain how their personalities may have contributed to the murder.

Both men were strong-willed and . . .

Part 5
In this part you describe the murder and consider who was to blame.

In the end Henry . . .

▼ DISCUSS

Who won in the end?
Becket was dead but did that mean he had lost? A year after Becket's death Henry was forced to come to Canterbury where he was flogged by monks as a punishment. In 1173 the Pope made Becket a saint. Pilgrims flocked to Becket's tomb at Canterbury, and still do. Eighty churches and two hospitals were named after Becket. The King kept the power to appoint bishops but the clergy were still tried in Church courts.

The murder did not sort out problems between the Church and the king. They would continue for centuries – a story you will pick up in later parts of your history course.

2 Who do you think had won in the long term?
3 Give Henry points out of 10 for how well he dealt with the problem.

Who were stronger – kings or barons? ▼

In the Middle Ages kings often had difficulty controlling their most powerful lords – the barons. On pages 87–91 you will look at the way kings and barons used castles in their wars with each other and you will plan a castle siege.

Kings needed barons to help them control the country. Barons were powerful lords. They controlled large areas of England and in these areas they could behave like little kings. Often they did not agree with the way the king was running the country. Sometimes this led to arguments and fighting. Many medieval kings faced REBELLIONS by their barons.

▼ **SOURCE 1** *The complaints barons made about kings*

The King is not running the country properly. He should listen to our advice much more.

The King is charging us too much tax.

The King is treating us unfairly, for example, he arrests barons and puts them in prison without a trial.

The King is too weak. We need a stronger king.

The King has been defeated in wars with other kings.

WHO WERE STRONGER – KINGS OR BARONS?

Kings, barons and castles

Barons usually controlled their part of England from castles. You will probably remember that William the Conqueror used castles to conquer and control England. At first they were made of wood but soon barons started making strong castles of stone.

In the twelfth century, castles became very important. When Henry I died in 1135, his nephew Stephen seized the throne. Many English barons would not accept him as King and twenty years of warfare followed. It was a dangerous time to be living in England. It is this time of 'anarchy' that gives many people the impression of the Middle Ages as such a violent and dangerous time. All over England barons built, improved and strengthened their castles to resist attacks. Different ways were used to attack a castle as you can see in Source 4. But it was almost impossible to capture a castle. You could lose so many soldiers in the process that the castles have been described as 'killing machines'.

Henry II came to the throne in 1154. Henry was a strong king and kept his barons under control. He had a large number of the barons' castles destroyed.

But the peace between kings and barons was not to last. Some 60 years later, King John went to war with his barons and in 1215 was forced to agree the Magna Carta (the Great Charter). This was the first document to set out the rights and freedoms of English people, for instance, freemen were not allowed to be put in prison without a trial.

▲ **SOURCE 2** *Early stone castles had square towers*

▲ **SOURCE 3** *Two of the main improvements to castles were the building of round towers and moats*

trebuchet
(for throwing stones)

siege tower

crossbow

scaling
ladders

mine

fire

battering ram

▲ **SOURCE 4** *Ways of attacking a castle*

▼ ACTIVITY

1 Match up these descriptions with the different ways of attacking a castle shown in Source 4.

This was used to punch holes in doors and walls.

This allowed attackers to climb the walls.

This was used to dig under the walls, particularly of a square tower, then set fire to the wooden props holding up the tunnel so that the walls collapsed.

Burning arrows were fired to set wooden doors or buildings inside the castle alight.

This allowed attackers to get close to walls and run across the top of them.

This fired stones and rocks into or against the castle to cause damage.

This allowed attackers to shoot more accurately at defenders on walls.

2 Look at Source 3. Work out why round towers were an improvement on square ones.

3 How do you think you could get a siege tower across a moat?

▼ RESEARCH

4 Find out more about the Magna Carta and why some people today regard it as very important. Your teacher will give you some hints about where to look.

Can you plan a castle siege?

The siege of Kenilworth

The year is 1265. Henry III is a weak king. His barons, led by Simon de Montfort, rebelled against him and defeated him.

For a year they have tried to rule England. But Simon is now dead and the rest of the rebels have fled to Kenilworth Castle, the strongest, best defended castle in the country. Can Henry capture it?

Henry orders siege engines and siege towers from different parts of the country, and also 30,000 crossbows and 2500 barricades. One of the siege towers is called 'the bear'. Barges are sent from Chester to be used to cross the lake.

Despite all these weapons, Henry fails to break the defences of Kenilworth. Two siege towers, each carrying 100 crossbow men, are destroyed by a catapult used by the castle's defenders. The siege lasts from Easter to December 1266. Will only starvation force the defenders to surrender?

▼ **SOURCE 5** *An archaeologist's plan of Kenilworth today. It shows what is left of the castle, and where the outer walls and barbican are believed to have been*

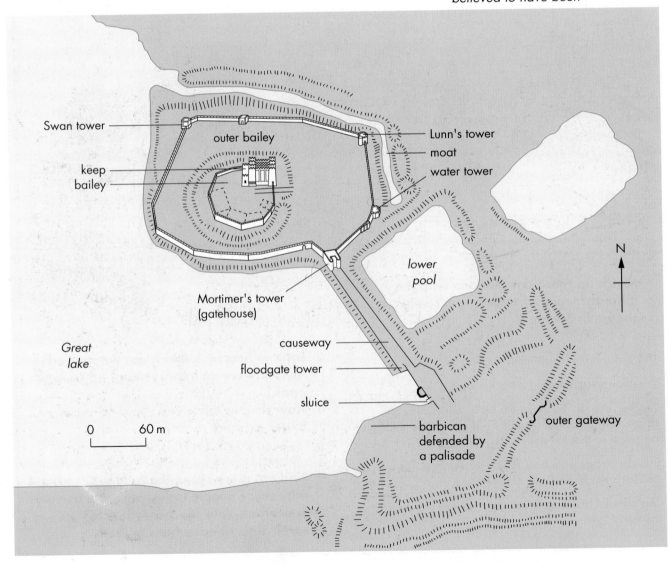

▼ ACTIVITY

Can you do better than Henry? Working in pairs or small groups, your task is to plan the best way of attacking Kenilworth. Use the drawing of the castle in Source 5 to help you plan. It is not easy – the castle is surrounded by water.

1   Choose the weapons and engines you want to use from Source 4 on page 89 and explain why you chose those items rather than others.

2   Draw up your plan of attack. Your teacher will give you a plan of Kenilworth to write down your ideas.

Think about:

- the way you are going to approach the castle
- how you are going to break in
- whether you are going to put all your effort into attacking one part of the castle, like the entrance, or whether you are going to attack in several different places at once
- how you are going to deal with the problem of the surrounding water.

3   When you have drawn up your final plan of attack, explain why you think it will work.

The Peasants' Revolt

The vast majority of the population in the Middle Ages were peasants and most of the time they were powerless. However, they could cause a lot of trouble if they got out of control. On pages 92–100 you are going to investigate why the peasants rose up against the young King Richard II in 1381 and find out what happened to them.

Why did the peasants revolt?

You will remember the peasants complaining about what they had to do for their lords (look back at page 40) and the situation after the Black Death (page 76). Well, in 1381, they were complaining much more, as you can see below.

> Nobody should be a villein. We should not have to do labour services for the lord of the manor. Everybody should be a freeman.

> Things got better after the Black Death in 1348. Because there were so few of us they started to pay us much better wages. But then they tried to force wages down to the same as they were before the Black Death.

> It wouldn't be so bad if we didn't have to pay these new Poll Taxes – 1377, 1379 and now 1381. Everybody over 15 has to pay 4 pence – and it's the same amount whether you are rich or poor . . . but some of the richest lords don't have to pay at all. Is that fair?

> And what are all these taxes for? Wars that have got nothing to do with us!

> Some lords are still making us do labour services like ploughing and harvesting, but won't pay us. I've had enough of it.

> The latest Poll Tax is worse than the others. The King's men are coming to make sure everybody pays up. People will not be able to hide like they did in the past. Everybody will have to pay.

So ... in 1381 a large group of peasants from different parts of the south east of England set off to London, to protest ...

To our sovereign King Richard

> The rich have wines, spices, and fine bread, while we have only rye and water. It is by our labour that they can live so well. We are called slaves, and if we do not perform our services we are beaten. Let us go to the King, he is young, and from him we may receive a favourable answer.

▼ **SOURCE 1** *A sermon by the peasants' leader, John Ball*

▼ **ACTIVITY**

1 **Which of the reasons for the peasants' anger had:**
   a) been annoying them for quite a few years
   b) made them particularly angry in the last two or three years?

2 **What is John Ball saying in Source 1 about:**
   a) what the rich people had
   b) how well they lived
   c) how the peasants were treated?

3 **Working in groups, pretend you are a group of villeins who want to complain to the King. You find an old priest who can write and ask him to write a letter to the young King Richard telling him why you're so angry and what you want him to do.**

THE PEASANTS' REVOLT

How did the revolt start?

▼ **SOURCE 2** *An extract from an account written by a monk in York in 1399*

In Essex

At Brampton in Essex, Thomas Brampton demanded a new payment of taxes from the people, who said they would not pay a penny more. Thomas ordered the men to be arrested. Then the COMMONS said they had already paid the tax, and rose up against him and tried to kill Thomas. They then went from place to place to stir up other folk.

In Kent

And at this moment [30 May 1381] a tax collector was sent to Kent, but he was turned back by the commons. And after this the commons of Kent gathered together in great numbers without a head or chieftain and on the Friday [4 June] came to Dartford. On the next Friday they came to Rochester. They then took their way to Maidstone, where they made Wat Tyler their chief. And on the Monday next they came to Canterbury. After cutting off the heads of three traitors, they took 500 men of the town with them to London, but left the rest to guard the town.

To London

At this time the commons had as their adviser an evil priest named Sir John Ball. A fit reward he got later, when he was hung, drawn and quartered. The commons went to many places and gathered 60,000 men. On their way to London they burned the manors of the Duke of Lancaster to the ground, because they hated him. When the King heard of these doings, he sent his messengers to them, asking why they were doing this. And they answered that they had risen to rescue him from traitors. The King agreed to meet them at Blackheath the next day.

The King was on his way, but turned back when his advisers warned him not to trust the commons.

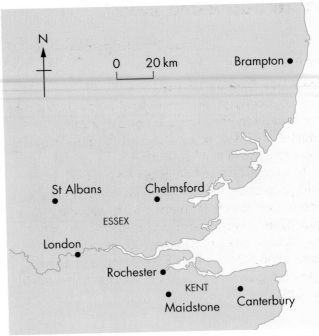

▲ **SOURCE 3** *A map of south-east England in 1381*

What happened next?

▼ **SOURCE 5** *An extract from an account written by a monk in York in 1399*

Into the City of London

The commons of Kent came to Southwark, and at the same time the commons of Essex came to Lambeth, where they ransacked the buildings of the Archbishop of Canterbury.

The commons of Kent went on to London Bridge to pass into the city. The commons of Southwark rose with them, and forced the guards to lower the drawbridge. The commons from Essex entered through Ald Gate. They came at the Duke of Lancaster's palace, broke open the gates and burnt all the buildings within the gates.

Mile End

The next day the commons from Kent and Essex met the King at Mile End. They asked that no men should be villeins. The King proclaimed that they should be free and pardoned them. The commons from Essex went home, but Wat Tyler and some men then made their way to the Tower, where they cut the Archbishop's head off and paraded it through the streets, on a wooden pole. That night they murdered some 140 people, and there were hideous cries and horrible tumult all through the night.

The King told all the commons to meet him at Smithfield the next day.

▼ **SOURCE 4** *John Ball leading the peasants. An illustration by a French artist painted some time after the event*

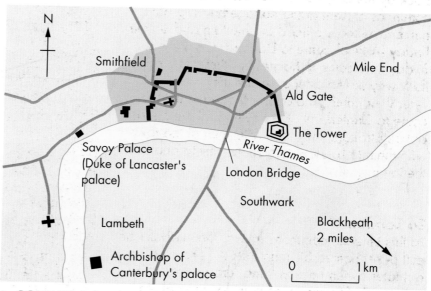

▲ **SOURCE 6** *London in 1381*

▼ **ACTIVITY**

1. On a copy of the maps of south-east England and London (Sources 3 and 6), make notes about what happened at different places.
2. Do you think the monk who wrote the extracts in Sources 2 and 5 was on the King's side?
3. a) How are the peasants dressed in Source 4?
   b) Do you think they would have really looked like this?

THE PEASANTS' REVOLT

What should King Richard do?

Richard II was only 14 at the time of the Peasants' Revolt. He was in a very tricky situation. Around him London was full of peasants, many of whom were drunk and rampaging through the streets. Several houses were on fire. Important royal officials, including the Archbishop of Canterbury and the Chancellor of England, had been killed, along with over a hundred other people.

▼ **SOURCE 7** *The peasants rampaging through London*

What should the King do?

You are one of King Richard's advisers. You meet to discuss what to do. There are things you need to take into account before you reach a decision. Would you advise the King to:

a) **give the peasants what they want. Wat Tyler, their leader, is not only demanding freedom for all men, but also that Church land should be given to the people**

b) **fight it out with the peasants. He could call on Londoners to support him**

c) **flee from London to somewhere safe**

d) **trick the peasants and play for time. He could pretend to give the peasants what they want and persuade them to go home. Later he could crush them**

e) **do something else. What ideas do you have about what he should do?**

Hurry Up!

You do not have much time to make your decision – the peasants are at the gates and you have to meet them at Smithfield tomorrow.

Write down the reasons why you chose one particular course of action and why you rejected the others.

If he shows weakness, the lords will desert him and look for another king.

He must have the support of the lords to remain King.

King Richard's advisers

The lords are furious about this situation. They are demanding that the peasants are brought under control.

He does not have enough soldiers to deal with the peasants.

He can't even call on loyal Londoners to help him. Many of them have joined in the revolt.

Death at Smithfield – you be Richard's judge

A version of events in June 1381

A version of events in June 1381

PEASANTS BETRAYED!

London, 15 June 1381
Today King Richard proved what a coward and trickster he is. Hiding behind bodyguards, Richard played his treacherous part in the bloody murder of Wat Tyler. Tyler agreed to the meeting because he believed the King was going to help put right the evils which made life a misery for so many ordinary people. But Richard went back on all the promises he had made to help the people.

In good faith Wat rode across to speak with the King, but was immediately surrounded by soldiers. Out of sight of the peasants, the bloodthirsty Mayor of London hacked down Tyler as he spat out some of the drink he had been given. It is not clear whether the drink had been tampered with.

The King rode up to the peasants. He told them to follow him, and he would see they got home safely, but they soon found themselves surrounded by soldiers.

BRAVE KING BEATS REBELS!

London, 15 June 1381
Today saw great celebrations after brave fourteen-year-old King Richard led his men to a brilliant victory over the peasant rebels who had brought death and destruction to the city.

With courage and majesty, the King rode to Smithfield with his trusted followers to meet an army of 20,000 angry rebels. Tyler advanced to the King, dagger in hand, and spat at him. He then stabbed the Mayor of London in the stomach. The Mayor bravely struck back with his sword and Tyler fell to the ground, screaming for revenge. King Richard calmly strode forward to the peasants and ordered them to obey him. Surprised, they followed him to nearby fields, where they surrendered. The King then let them go home safely.

▲ **SOURCE 8** *This picture was painted about 60 years after the revolt. It shows Richard twice. On the left-hand side he is raising his hand as Wat Tyler is struck down. On the right he is speaking with the rebels*

Bravery or betrayal?

Richard met the peasants at Smithfield on June 15. The made-up reports on the opposite page give different versions of what might have happened. Sources 9 and 10 agree with one of the versions.

Froissart records that when the peasants saw that Wat had been struck down, they raised their bows ready to fire on the King's men. But Richard bravely rode over to them and said: 'Gentlemen, you have no other leader but me. I am your King. Keep the peace.' When they saw and heard the King speak, most of the crowd were ashamed and the more peaceful began to disperse.

The commons were arrayed in battle formation in great numbers. Tyler dismounted, carrying his dagger. He called for some water and rinsed his mouth in a very rude disgusting fashion in front of the King. One of the King's men called out that Tyler was the greatest robber in Kent.

Tyler then made to strike the man with his dagger. The Mayor of London tried to arrest him, and because of this Wat stabbed the Mayor with his dagger in the stomach, But the Mayor, as it pleased God, was wearing armour, and drew his cutlass and gave Wat a deep cut on the neck, and then a great cut on the head.

▼ ACTIVITY

1 **Which version of the story do Sources 9 and 10 agree with?**
2 **Some historians do not think this version is true. They say that all the accounts of the meeting at Smithfield were written by people who were on the King's side. The statements below give different views about the meeting at Smithfield. Sort them into two groups:**

   - **statements that could be used to support the view that there was a plot to kill Wat, or**
   - **statements that could be used to support the view that Wat was at fault and the King was brave.**

The Mayor of London and the King's advisers knew that a revolt in France in 1358 had been stopped when its leader had been killed.

Wat Tyler was too sure of himself. He thought that he was in control because he had so many men.

He behaved rudely on purpose to show that he could do what he wanted – asking for a drink and then spitting it out.

One of the King's men deliberately insulted Wat so that he would behave violently. Then the mayor could stab him.

The Mayor of London struck Wat down because he was behaving in a rude and threatening way with a dagger in his hand.

King Richard realised that many people could get killed and bravely went over to the peasants to tell them to leave.

It is very unlikely that a young boy such as Richard would have ridden straight over to the peasants on his own. It was part of a plan.

Afterwards King Richard went back on all his promises to pardon the peasants and make them freemen.

▼ DISCUSS

3 **Give Richard points out of 10 for how well he dealt with the peasants.**

THE PEASANTS' REVOLT

▼ ACTIVITY

No accounts of the Peasants' Revolt have survived which tell the story of what happened from the peasants' point of view. Few, if any, peasants could write and even then it is unlikely that someone would have kept their writings in a safe place for future generations.

But what if historians did discover a diary kept by a peasant from Kent who joined Wat Tyler in the revolt? Write five extracts from this diary. You can use the suggestions here or choose your own episodes to write about. When you have finished, make your document look like an old one.

Your teacher will tell you how to do this.

> **30 May 1381**
> My village was up in arms about the Poll Tax. When the tax inspector arrived, we . . .
>
> I and several villagers decided to march to Maidstone. We were in good spirits. We . . .

> **5 June**
> We found the people of Maidstone in a right old state. Many people had come in from the villages nearby. No one knew what to do. Then one man, by the name of Wat Tyler, made himself known. Tyler said . . .
>
> We also listened to a speech by a priest, John Ball. He told us that . . .

> **13 June**
> We are in London. I have never been so far from home in my life. Great news — Londoners have joined us and let us into the city. But things have got out of control. There are . . .

> **14 June**
> I can't believe it. We have seen young King Richard at Mile End. He . . .

> **15 June**
> This has been a sad and terrible day. We came to Smithfield thinking we had won. But . . .

HOW DID IT ALL END?

It ended badly for the peasants. Their leaders were rounded up and hung. John Ball was hung, drawn and quartered. King Richard went back on his promises and the peasants gained virtually nothing.

BUT ...

it did make the rich and powerful more careful about how they treated the peasants and within 50 years the peasants had got much of what they wanted, for example, the end of labour services ... so maybe the Peasants' Revolt was not such a failure after all.

Review: Problems facing medieval kings

It was not always easy being a king in the Middle Ages. Kings had to deal with problems that threatened their powers and even their lives. You have investigated three areas where different medieval kings found themselves in very difficult situations. In the pictures below the King is dreaming – or having nightmares – about his problems.

Write down what you think might be going on in the King's dreams. You might start like this:

I had a terrible dream last night. I dreamt that . . .

The barons

English kings could not rule the country properly without the co-operation of the barons. They were very powerful and could not always be trusted.

The Church

English kings were not complete masters of their lands for another reason – the Catholic Church. This was under the control of the Pope in Rome. Disputes broke out between the King and the Church over who was more important.

The peasants

The vast majority of people in England were peasants who worked on the land. Their lives were hard, and famine and starvation were never far away. This meant there was always the danger of uprisings.

Review: What were the Middle Ages really like?

At the beginning of this course you looked at the good and bad things about the Middle Ages. Now that you have become an expert in this period you will have seen that in some ways the Middle Ages were violent, but in other ways they were peaceful. Some people were clever and some people were cruel.

1   Look at the word bubbles on this page. What evidence could each speaker use to support their views?

The Middle Ages were peaceful

Life in the Middle Ages was dangerous

People in the Middle Ages were cruel

2 Would you like to have lived in the Middle Ages? Give at least five reasons for your answer.

3 Now use your answers to questions 1 and 2 to plan a class display about the Middle Ages.

Glossary

AD   stands for *Anno Domini* which means 'in the year of the Lord'. It is used for dates after the birth of Christ

ANGLO-SAXONS   people from Germany who ruled England from the fifth century until 1066

ARCHAEOLOGIST   person who studies past peoples, usually by digging for remains they have left behind, such as buildings or tools. These remains are called ARCHAEOLOGICAL evidence

ARCHBISHOP   a powerful Church leader

BAILIFF   a medieval manor official appointed by the lord (see REEVE and STEWARD)

BARON   a powerful lord who was granted land by the king (see FEUDAL SYSTEM)

BC   Before Christ. BC years are counted backwards from the birth of Christ, so 200BC came before 100BC

BISHOP   a man in charge of the affairs of the Christian Church over a large area called a diocese

BOON-WORK   see WEEK-WORK

CANDLEMAS   a feast with a blessing of candles to celebrate the Virgin Mary (2nd February)

CHARTER   a medieval document setting out the rights of a town or a group of people

CLERGY   all the people such as priests, monks, nuns who have been appointed to perform religious duties in the Christian Church

COMMONS   ordinary people who are not lords or knights

DEMESNE   the part of the MANOR farmed by the lord in the Middle Ages

EARL   a powerful nobleman

ESTATE   a large area of land owned by a lord or important churchman

FREEMAN   a peasant who had achieved some freedom from the lord (see VILLEIN)

GUILD   an association of merchants, or workers with a particular craft

INVADE   to bring an army into a country to try and control it

JURY   a group of people who hear evidence in a court and decide the verdict

KNIGHT   a lord who was granted land by a baron in return for support and army service

LATIN   official language of the Roman Empire

MANOR   the area controlled by a medieval lord, usually only one village

MANUSCRIPT   handwritten book, often with brightly coloured illustrations

MEDIEVAL   dating from the Middle Ages. In this book, the period called medieval is about AD1000–1500

MERCHANT   person who trades in goods, often from foreign countries

PEASANT   the vast majority of poor people in medieval villages, who worked on the land

PILGRIMAGE   journey to a holy place, such as a SHRINE

PLAGUE   a disease which affects large numbers of people

PRIEST   a man in charge of religious ceremonies. In Christian countries, he is responsible for a particular village or parish

REBELLION   people fighting against their rulers

REEVE   a medieval manor official – one of the villagers, and elected by them (see BAILIFF and STEWARD)

REVOLT   trying to overthrow the king or person in power

SHERIFF   official appointed by the king, responsible for keeping law and order in medieval Britain

SHRINE   holy place, usually sacred to a god or a saint

STEWARD   official who ran the lord's manor for him in the Middle Ages (see BAILIFF and REEVE)

TITHE   tax which medieval people had to pay to the village priest: one tenth of their farm produce

VIKINGS   Scandinavians who raided and settled in the south and east of Britain during the ninth and tenth centuries

VILLEIN   a peasant who was under the control of the lord of the manor in the Middle Ages. A villein could buy his freedom and become a FREEMAN

WEEK-WORK   the services, fixed by tradition, that all medieval VILLEINS had to give to the lord. BOON-WORK was the extra service the peasant did for the lord when the manor needed it

Index

owledgements

...duced by kind permission of:

...n Library; **p.v** *top* Michael Holford, *centre* British Library, ...ritish Library; **p.2** *clockwise from left* Hulton Getty, The Pierpont ...n Library, New York M763 f.19v, British Library; **p.3** *top* Bodleian ...ary, Oxford Ms.Rawl.D.410f.1r, *bottom* British Library; **p.4** *top* Hulton ...etty, *bottom* British Library; **p.5** *top* Michael Holford, *middle* The Master and Fellows of Trinity College Cambridge, *bottom* Bodleian Library, Oxford Ms.Bodl.264f.121v; **p.6** *top* Michael Holford, *middle, far left* English Heritage, *middle, second left* Bridgeman Art Library, *bottom* British Library; **pp.7; 10; 11; 17; 18** *all* Michael Holford; **p.23** The Dean and Chapter of Durham; **p.28** English Heritage; **p.31** British Library; **p.32** Cambridge University Collection of Air Photographs: copyright reserved; **p.33** English Heritage; **p.34** Peter Dunn/English Heritage; **pp.36–37** *clockwise from top* British Library, Bodleian Library, Oxford Ms.Bodl.763f.80r, British Library; **p.38** *top* Hulton Getty, *middle* AA Picture Library, *bottom* British Library; **p.39** British Library; **p.41** *both* British Library; **p.43** *top left* British Library, *top right* British Library, *middle* Bridgeman Art Library, *bottom* British Library; **p.44** British Library; **p.45** British Library; **p.46** Peter Dunn/English Heritage; **p.49** Bridgeman Art Library; **P.54** Michael Holford; **p.58** Michael Holford; **p.65** *clockwise from left* Scala Italy, British Library, British Library; **p.74** Scala Italy; **p.79** The visions dreamt by King Henry I in Normandy in 1130, inserted c.1140 by John of Worcester into the chronicle begun by Florence of Worcester (d.1118) c.1130-40 (parchment) Corpus Christi College, Oxford/Bridgeman Art Library; **p.80** British Library; **p.88** English Heritage; **p.94–5** British Library; **p.98** British Library; **p.101** as p.79.

Every effort has been made to contact copyright holders, but if any have been inadvertantly overlooked the Publishers will be pleased to make the necessary arrangement at the earliest opportunity.